6/92

A Horse in Your Backyard

A First-Time Owner's Primer of Horse Keeping

VIRGINIA PHELPS CLEMENS

PRENTICE
HALL PRESS
EQUESTRIAN
BOOKS

New York   London   Toronto   Sydney   Tokyo   Singapore

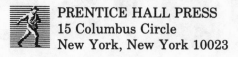 PRENTICE HALL PRESS
15 Columbus Circle
New York, New York 10023

PRENTICE HALL PRESS and colophons are registered
trademarks of Simon & Schuster Inc.

Library of Congress Cataloging-in-Publication Data

Clemens, Virginia Phelps.
    A horse in your backyard: a first-time owner's primer of horse
keeping / by Virginia Phelps Clemens.
        p.   cm.
    Includes bibliographical references and index.
    Summary : Discusses the selection and care of a young rider's
first horse.
    ISBN 0-13-395088-3
    1. Horses—Juvenile literature. [1. Horses. 2. Horsemanship.]
I. Title.
SF302.C58   1991
636.1—dc20   90-46769
                                                            CIP
                                                            AC

Designed by Levavi & Levavi

Manufactured in the United States of America

10 9 8 7 6 5 4 3 2 1

First Edition

For my family and friends, both two and four legged. With special thanks to my husband, Doug; Sharon Ross; Peter Blauner, D.V.M.; S. C. Eaton for the drawings; and my editor, Steven Price.

Contents

Introduction

Is there a horse in your backyard? Or is your family planning to add an equine to its growing menagerie of pets in the near future?

If so, as a parent of a child begging for a horse of his or her own, you must have numerous questions, and possibly no one to answer them.

The information included in this book—from horse owners, stable managers, veterinarians, blacksmiths, feed dealers, and tack shop owners—should answer all your questions and quite probably many you never considered.

Congratulations for trying to find out the best way to care for your family's new pet. Your children may have promised to take care of your first horse, but emergencies arise and situations occur when a parent must step in to help or take over. Unfortunately, too many horse owners, old and new, take for granted that a horse will do quite well with no more care than they give a dog or cat. After all, the mustangs on the plains have no one to feed, groom, or clean up after them.

Horses suffer in silence. Through ignorance, carelessness, selfishness, and even an overabundance of kindness at the wrong time (rarely deliberate cruelty), too many do suffer.

Even horse experts have a variety of opinions and methods on caring, selecting, training, and riding a horse. To use a hay net or hayrack, or just to throw the hay in a corner of the stall? To keep a halter on the horse when he is in the barn or out in the pasture? What feed and bedding do the best job? Knowledgeable horse owners often disagree.

A Horse in Your Backyard offers logical and easy-to-follow advice and hints for new horse owners with their first horse. But you must decide for yourself what works best with your horse and is most convenient for you and your family. What agrees with other equines may not be the ideal method for your pet, so let common sense take over, and don't be afraid to experiment a little, using the information in this book as a starting point.

Pros and Cons of Backyard Horse Keeping

So, you're thinking of buying a horse for your children? Their pleas have finally worn you down. You remember how much you wanted a horse at their age and never got one.

Or maybe you've always thought horses were beautiful and exciting, and after enduring some persuasive techniques from your youngsters, you now think this might be a good opportunity for everyone in the family to become acquainted with one. In fact, you might do some riding, too. Galloping across a field into the sunset has always been a secret fantasy.

Or maybe you've admired horses from afar—and liked it that way—but the pressure from your child or children is starting to crack your defense and dilute your arguments.

Any one of these descriptions might fit you, and maybe they all do.

In 1986, the American Horse Council in Washington, D.C., did a study on the "Economic Impact of the United States Horse Industry," which set the equine population in this country at 5.25 million—and growing!

One of the most popular sports in the United States today, horseback riding is also one of the most healthful, providing fresh air and vigorous exercise for its enthusiasts. More than 27 million people over the age of twelve ride horses each year.

And here's an additional benefit: A child who is mucking stalls, cleaning tack, scrubbing water buckets, and currying and brushing what seems like a mountain of horse hide—dust in her hair and nostrils, manure on her shoes, and saddle soap under her fingernails—hardly has the time or energy to get into mischief. And you will soon have a whole new set of friends—the parents of your youngster's riding pals.

KNOW YOUR OBLIGATIONS

Owning a horse and keeping it in your backyard will be quite an experience—both educational and stimulating—for your whole family. It will also require patience, perseverance, and, of course, plenty of muscle and just plain hard work.

A youngster getting a horse should be mature enough to recognize the work ahead and to have the stick-to-itiveness to keep up with the chores after the newness wears off.

To eliminate the everyday drudgery of caring for a horse, yet still be able to enjoy riding, you might decide to allow your child to rent a horse for an hour when the mood strikes him or her or to take weekly riding lessons. But if your family still wants a horse all its own, occasional riding is not the most satisfying arrangement. Those who only hire a horse by the hour miss the companionship and fun of knowing and having a horse for a friend.

The new pet's care may be the children's responsibility—remember how they promised to take care of it when asking for one?—but it is the parents' responsibility to make sure that the children feed, water, and care for the horse properly and regularly. Adult supervision is a must, no matter how mature and dependable your children are. A horse needs constant, daily attention and all family members should be willing to help. Although your children vowed to take care of the horse all by themselves, emergencies will occur.

A horse in the backyard is a hobby and an experience that the whole family should plan to share—and may have to whether they want to or not. A 900-plus-pound animal is a *big* job.

You as a parent should realize that after the novelty of owning a horse wears off, your youngster may need a little reminding of his obligation in the backyard. Homework piled high on the kitchen table or an invitation to a party will just have to wait until those stable chores are finished.

On the other hand, the laundry, a golf game, or a social function you planned to attend may also have to be delayed or canceled if your youngster is unavoidably detained at school or is ill and those stable chores need doing.

Vacation plans will now have to include who's going to care for your horse in the backyard. A dog or cat are easily taken to a boarding kennel, but reservations for a horse are an entirely different matter. However, you may have a friendly neighbor who happens to own a horse, too, and caring for an extra horse when another family is on vacation usually works out quite well. And sometimes you can find a nearby stable that will board your horse for a week or two if you have no knowledgeable horsey neighbors or friends you can rely on.

Although backyard horses are relatively cheap to buy, their upkeep can become quite a financial burden. The cost of hay, grain, bedding, services of a blacksmith and veterinarian, and equipment (saddle, blankets, brushes, pails, etc.—see chapters 4 and 5) mount up quickly and considerably.

Talk to a local stable manager and/or feed mill owner to find out the cost of hay, feed, and bedding in your area before you buy a horse and then realize you can't afford to keep him. Depending on what part of the country you live in, these costs will vary considerably. Even in the same area the price for a bale of hay fluctuates according to its weight, how good the growing season was, and whether it is alfalfa, timothy, clover, meadow grass, or a mixture. A 45-pound bale of timothy hay can cost between two and three dollars, but if storage and delivery charges are tacked on, the cost can be more.

PREPARATIONS FOR HORSE KEEPING

If your child has not had any hands-on riding experience (reading about it is not doing it!), contact a local riding school and make arrangements for riding lessons. Your neighborhood tack shop or veterinarian can probably recommend a reliable stable.

Allowing your youngster to learn to ride on his or her own without knowledgeable help is foolhardy and dangerous. In fact, if you have any desire to ride the new family pet, you, too, should take some lessons, either to brush up on your riding (remember being told, "Heads up, heels down," until you thought you would scream?) or to learn to ride from scratch. Your child should learn to ride English style rather than Western if both are available. The biggest difference is that English riders learn to post to the trot and, with more advanced lessons, they also learn to jump. Except for differences in position, the Western rider learns little that the English rider doesn't. Thus, it is much easier to change one's mind and go from English to Western than vice versa. However, if you're in an area where everyone rides Western and you have no desire to post or jump, then by all means learn to ride Western style.

Knowing how to ride, however, is only part of what is needed to become a conscientious horse owner. Riding lessons often include information about the care of horses, but if this is not covered, encourage your child to volunteer to help groom horses, muck out stalls, and clean tack to learn what it's really like to own a horse.

You as a parent should also watch, ask questions, or volunteer to help, too. The stable manager will probably welcome an extra hand, and you will be making a knowledgeable friend to whom you can turn for advice or help when you have your own horse.

Another alternative to buying a horse is first to lease one from an owner (such as a college student away at school) or to have your child share one with a friend. This way your youngster is able to ride more often with only half the expense of owning and, at the same time, learn about horses and horse-keeping duties.

Local 4-H and Pony Clubs are fine organizations for your child to consider joining. (Your local tack shop or veterinarian should be able to tell you who to contact in your

Before you buy a horse, your child should take riding lessons from a qualified instructor.

area about joining.) Their members are other youngsters—horse and pony owners their age with their shared interest—and they offer an opportunity for you to meet still more parents involved in the world of horses and children.

The primary focus of 4-H Clubs is on animal care; 4-H urges members to "learn by doing." Once a club has chosen its projects, such as the care of a horse, the members must periodically turn in reports and charts of their daily

Lessons often include information about the care of horses after you dismount.

progress—a good way of having methods of horse care evaluated.

Applicants for 4-H clubs must be at least nine years old. Depending on the individual, this is a good minimum age for a child to start riding lessons and learning how to care for a horse. A child of five may ride beautifully but just won't have the physical strength or size to muck out a stall, properly groom a horse, or even lift the saddle into place.

The Pony Club emphasizes all aspects of horsemanship and especially encourages improvement in riding through rallies, clinics, and a rider rating system. In order to advance to a higher rating, Pony Club members must pass both written and riding tests. The "three R's of Pony Club" refer to Reading, Riding, and Responsibility: reading to obtain the knowledge to properly care for and teach ponies and horses; riding safely and skillfully so members can pursue a healthy sport throughout their lives; and responsibility to care properly for a horse.

Speakers and demonstrators at meetings of both 4-H and Pony Clubs provide additional information on horse keeping. Your county agricultural agent and Society for the Prevention of Cruelty to Animals can also give advice on caring for a horse in your area.

BACKYARD SUITABILITY

Is your backyard suitable to keep a horse? An acre of land is enough for one horse, although the more room your horse has, the happier he will be. Less than an acre—and some horses have considerably less—will be adequate if the horse is given regular daily exercise.

To add to the horse's pasture area, you could have the barn and a small paddock in your backyard and rent a field for grazing from a neighbor. Land under power lines can sometimes be leased from the electric company for such a purpose, too.

Check with your local zoning office to see whether you have enough land to keep a horse legally on your property. Zoning requirements change as an area becomes more built up. Even though a neighbor has a horse, you may not be able to; the neighbor may have acquired his animal before the last zoning change was made.

Your insurance agent can tell you whether additional coverage is necessary. Most companies consider a backyard horse to be like any other pet; however, if it gets loose and causes damage to your neighbors' property too often and you make claim after claim, the company will probably send out an investigator to see what can be done. His or her recommendation (putting up a stronger fence, in this case) must be followed to avoid raising your rates or dropping your coverage. (A horse that bites or kicks will be compared to a dog that bites; it is recommended that such an animal be sold, for the safety of everyone.)

Where there is a horse there is also manure, and the removal of manure can be quite a problem. One horse produces a lot of manure—about 25 pounds a day! Again, there may be rules in your area regarding manure, and the amount you may store and how close to the property line the pile may be.

One Pennsylvania borough allows horse owners to keep no more than two wagonloads of manure on a property within its boundaries, a holdover from the town's horse-and-buggy days.

If you have only one horse—and strong persuasive powers—you can often arrange to distribute much of the manure among your neighbors for their gardens and compost piles. You'll still have plenty for your own use. (Remember to let the manure age before putting it around shrubbery, because fresh manure will burn the roots. A good time to work it into your garden is in the fall or winter when everything is dormant. By the time you are ready to plant in the spring the soil will be well fertilized.)

Often, mushroom growers, nurserymen, or farmers are able to use horse manure, although they may not be willing to pick up the manure from only one horse. (The amount is too little to bother hauling away.) A last resort is to pay to have it hauled away every month or so.

Is there someone in your neighborhood with whom you can ride? Are there trails and fields to use for riding? Riding alone will eventually become very boring, especially if you can only ride in circles in your ring or paddock every day. It's more fun to have a friend to share your horsey interest, to talk to and ride with along trails through woods and meadows.

Neighbors with strong objections to your keeping a horse in your backyard need to be educated and reassured. Tell them about your facilities and safety measures. Often they have had little or no experience with horses, outside of pony rides at a fair, and they fear that this huge monster of yours will get loose and attack them at their barbecue grill. Or a huge increase in horseflies will carry off their tiny toy poodle and drive them from their patio.

Children in the area must also be told about horses and cautioned about the dangers of being accidentally stepped on or knocked over. A good practice to enforce right from the beginning is to not allow any children on your property or near the horse without their parents unless you are there.

BOARDING

Would it be more convenient to board your horse at a local stable?

There are a variety of boarding arrangements available, depending on the stable you chose. "Rough board," or a bare stall, is the cheapest arrangement and may cost as little as $50 a month. It includes just the stall—box or straight.

A box stall is more expensive but gives the horse room to move about, while a straight stall is narrow (5 by 8 feet) and the horse is tied with just enough room to lie down. You provide your own feed and bedding and must visit the stable at least twice a day to clean the stall, water, feed, groom, and exercise your horse. A disadvantage here is that you usually have little or no place to store feed and bedding, so you must keep everything at home and haul it back and forth. You end up with your horse practically living out of the trunk or backseat of your car, an embarrassing situation when a guest climbs into your car, comments on that distinct horsey odor, and climbs out with wisps of hay clinging to her navy slacks or black wool coat.

"Full board" usually includes feed, bedding, stall cleaning, turnout, and sometimes grooming. Prices for this arrangement may exceed $800 or $900 a month depending on where you live. The more rural your area, the less expensive the board will be. With full board you usually only have to pay veterinarian and farrier bills and exercise your horse.

Services included in the monthly rent vary from stable to stable. Always check to see what is covered in the board and how much any extras will cost. Some stables that seem to be cheaper at first will add charges for every little service, such as worming or turning the horse out for exercise, so that you end up actually paying more. Ask other boarders who have been there for at least a few months their opinion of the horse care, and check with the local humane society to make sure the stable has a good record.

A stable with turnout paddocks or fenced-in pastures, where your horse can get out every day, is preferable to one where your horse is cooped up in his stall all the time. Turning your horse out will eliminate the necessity of everyday riding so he doesn't charge out of his stall like a wild stallion. Daily exercise is also good for the horse's "mental health."

The availability of riding rings and trails is another plus, and an indoor arena might be worth a higher boarding fee if you live in a northern climate with more severe winters. A riding instructor or trainer is usually associated with a large stable so that riding lessons can easily be arranged for your youngster without the hassle of trailering your horse elsewhere or finding someone to come to your barn.

Another advantage of boarding is that you can usually get a group rate on farrier and veterinary bills if all the horses are trimmed and shod and given their annual vaccinations at the same time. And full board also means that your horse will be properly looked after even if the weather is bad and you can't get to the stable or if you are away on vacation.

A way to save on expenses is for your youngster to do grooming or other chores at the stable in exchange for the horse's accommodations. Or you can allow your horse to be used by other riders who are taking lessons or hiring a mount for an hour's ride. This arrangement will help to keep him exercised if your child can't ride regularly.

The disadvantage of letting your horse be ridden by others is that he may be rented out on weekends and after school when your family wants to ride him. And you can't be sure how he is going to be treated.

CONCLUSION

If, after weighing all the factors involved in owning a horse and keeping it in your backyard, you still decide to go ahead with your idea, take things slowly. Don't rush into any purchase or commitment you may later regret. A little common sense used in planning for your new pet will eliminate unnecessary headaches. Don't buy a horse until your facilities—barn and paddock—are ready, or you'll have to spend additional funds on boarding until they are completed.

Remember, your horse should always come first, in spite of personal inconvenience and discomfort. Hearing a nicker as you approach the barn, watching your child get her first ribbon at a local horse show, or being able to daydream on your horse's sunbaked back as he grazes in a field will be well worth the effort and sacrifices you make for him.

Backyard to Barnyard

Converting your backyard into a barnyard may be fairly simple, depending on the facilities already there and the area you have available.

A garage or other unused building may need only a few alterations for conversion into a stall. However, if the structure does need a major overhaul, you may find it easier and cheaper to start all over and build a new barn in another location.

DRAW A DIAGRAM

Your first step will be to map out your allotted acreage, deciding where your barn, paddock, and manure pile should be placed.

Your local zoning office can tell you whether your barn or fence has to be a stipulated distance from a neighbor's property line. The manure pile may also have restrictions on its location, size, and manner of storage, as well as whether it must be fenced in or covered.

A barn is not an absolute necessity for a horse accustomed to your area's weather, but a shelter of some kind is essential. An unclipped (see chapter 6), healthy horse will do fine with a three-sided lean-to that protects him from winter winds and summer sun and flies. However, despite the extra expense, a barn with storage room will be more comfortable for your pet and more convenient for you. Remember too that the attractiveness of your barn will be a plus for possible resale of your property later.

Plan on an area of at least 12 by 20 feet for a one-horse stable and adjoining tack room. You may want to build an extra stall right away because a one-horse family often becomes a two-or-more-horse family. It's cheaper to plan for the future when the initial building is done, and you will find that there is always a need for more storage space.

At the very least, choose a floor plan and location for your barn that will allow you to add on a stall or two in the future. Check your local building codes to make sure everything, such as location or materials used, is legal.

Water and electricity in your new barn are well worth the extra expense, but a heating system is unnecessary even in the coldest of climates. A horse's body throws off so much heat that even after a cold winter night, a well-insulated barn housing one horse will actually feel warm in the morning.

The barn should be close enough to your house for accessibility in bad weather. In fact, some horse owners in northern areas have made the barn an extension of their house (where zoning laws permit it) so they don't have to go outside to feed and clean. A must here is to keep a clean barn so the horsey odors don't infiltrate the house. (*Eau de manure* never added to a dinner party that I know of.)

When choosing a site know how the winds blow and where the sun rises and sets so you can take advantage of nature's heating system in the winter and its air conditioning in the summer. A site approximately 50 yards downwind (in most parts of the country this is to the east) of your home is sufficient.

The barn door should face toward the south or southeast for extra warmth and protection. Notice from which direction the cold winds of winter sweep across your property. Build your barn so that the doors and windows are on the sides away from these icy blasts. Likewise, if you live in an area where heat and sun are more of a problem you should take advantage of cooling breezes and shade trees.

Build your barn inside the paddock or field in a corner or along one side so that the stall door opens out into the fenced area. With this arrangement you can treat your barn

Build your barn so one door opens out into a fenced-in area.

like a run-in shed and allow the horse to go in and out as he pleases. This saves on stall cleaning and gives the horse the option of getting out of bad weather. Also, if your horse gets loose in the barn and runs out he will have no place to go.

Also plan for trailer-wide driveways (at least 12 feet wide) and turnarounds for feed and hay trucks making deliveries. Horse trailers need more room to maneuver, too.

A tack room or storage area will be a convenience for you and will eliminate hauling your tack, and grooming and cleaning equipment back and forth from your house or garage to the barn. A hayloft and places to store grain and bedding are also necessities.

BARN

Your barn should be dry and airy, but not drafty, and built on a high, well-drained site so water will run away from it. A damp, dark, low stable is a breeding ground for the germs that cause colds, coughs, and rheumatism.

When choosing the materials to be used in the construction of your barn, you should consider their cost, durability, attractiveness, fire resistance, and maintenance. Cost can range from a few hundred dollars for an inexpensive but adequate facility that you and your family build yourselves to several thousand dollars for a custom-designed showplace.

Some materials used for barns include wood (use hardwoods, such as oak, because horses chew and even eat soft woods such as pine); metal; masonry, including concrete, brick, and stone, as well as cinder, concrete, or pumice block; and plastics. Prefabricated wooden barns, which have frames that are preassembled at the factory before installation, are also quite popular.

The roof should have an overhang of at least 3 feet in front and back with gutters directing rainwater away from the barn's foundation. An overhang of 6 or more feet in front will give you adequate room to crosstie your horse for grooming. The roof should be of wood covered with either shingles or metal sheeting with a layer of tar paper to muffle the sound of rain or hail.

A cupola on the roof and a fan in the hayloft above the stall will help to ventilate your barn. They will draw hot air up through an open hay drop above the stall. Leave the weather vane off your roof, however, because they attract lightning.

Your barn's foundation should be deep enough to keep water and rodents from getting underneath. Walls should fit tight to the floor so there are no drafts on a horse's feet and legs or back when he is lying down.

Aluminum siding, which is excellent insulation for walls, will add to the barn's appearance, as will nontoxic paint. However, aluminum siding will dent if a horse kicks it so this material is best restricted to areas the horse can't reach.

A tree or two for shade and shrubbery around the barn will also enhance its beauty. But they, too, must not be within the horse's reach, because he will chew the bark, eat the leaves and branches, and finally pull the stump right out of the ground.

BARN'S INTERIOR

A floor plan is the first step before construction. A simple one-stall stable with a storage room to one side doesn't need much of a diagram. But if you're building more than one stall with a tack room, feed storage area, and an aisle, a little more thought has to go into the plan. A good, efficient floor plan saves steps and time. An experienced barn builder can help you with ideas.

Your horse's stall should have enough room for him to move about freely, and it should accommodate receptacles for feed, water, and a salt block. It is false economy to scrimp on a stall, so plan on a good-sized box—8 by 8 feet for a small pony, 10 by 10 for a large pony, 12 by 12 for a horse— and you will have less cleaning and less wear and tear inside, as well as a more contented horse. Since horses often nap while standing, many people don't realize that if horses have the room, they prefer to lie down to sleep.

A bored and cramped horse, particularly one that is high-strung and nervous, can develop bad habits to relieve nervous energy if he is cooped up in a small stall. You will also appreciate the extra footage if this is the only covered area in which you can groom your horse in bad weather.

A minimum ceiling height of 10 feet and door height of 7 feet are additional safety measures, for they reduce the chances of a rearing horse striking his head.

The stall's door should swing outward or slide to the side. The doorway should be at least 3, preferably 4, feet wide. If a horse becomes ill and lies down next to the door, you won't be able to get to him if the door swings inward and his body is blocking it. The popular Dutch door is a good choice; the top half can be opened for light and air, while the lower half keeps the horse inside.

Screens for the entire stall door—for summer use—are available from horse equipment stores and catalogs. They should be large enough to prevent your horse from going under or over them.

A window opposite the stall door will provide cross ventilation when cool breezes are a premium on hot summer days. The window should swing outward, and if glass panes are used, they should be covered on the inside with heavy screening or bars to prevent your horse from pushing them out and injuring himself on the broken glass.

The floor of the stall will be an important decision. All materials have definite pros and cons, but several inches of packed clay on top of a gravel foundation for drainage is recommended most often. It both cushions a horse's weight and absorbs moisture best. Pawing, however, will gouge out holes and gullies that periodically have to be filled in and leveled. Depending on the occupant of the stall, some floors soon resemble miniature roller coasters.

A hard dirt floor is also easy on a horse's legs, but not as absorbent as packed clay, and it also has to be smoothed over when it hollows out. Wooden floorboards retain moisture and odors, are slippery when wet, and will eventually rot through, with disastrous consequences if your horse's leg slips down between the splintering boards.

Concrete is considered perfectly acceptable by some people because it is easy to clean. But it is expensive and it is very hard on a horse's legs if he is standing in his stall for long periods of time. (The same drawbacks apply to asphalt and blacktop.) If you decide on a concrete floor, be sure to rough it up a little so it won't be slippery, and use extra-thick bedding for padding. Heavy rubber mats can also be used under the bedding for extra cushioning. A gradual slope of 1 inch every 3 feet toward the back of the stall to the outside will allow for drainage.

A concrete floor for tack room and storage area is definitely recommended, since concrete will aid in keeping rodents from tunneling underneath and into the feed bins. (Your friendly barn cat is another way to keep the rat and mouse population under control, and you will give your horse some companionship and a deserving cat a good home.)

Walls should be solid and kickproof, preferably 2 by 12-inch oak planks. Wood gives a little if kicked, but concrete blocks and other similar materials don't and thus may injure your horse's legs if he kicks them.

Walls between stalls should be high enough to keep drafts off your horse's back, but not so high that he cannot see his neighbor (about 4½ to 5 feet high). Bars, pipe, or chain-link fencing are good choices and should be installed from the top of the dividing walls to the ceiling to prevent the horses from reaching over and nipping each other.

The open area in the upper half of the walls encourages good air circulation and allows you to see in and the horse to see out. Poor ventilation is a real threat to a horse's respiratory health because trapped air becomes stagnant and damp, an ideal breeding ground for germs and lung pollutants.

The wall between the stall and the feed room should be solid from floor to ceiling so there is absolutely no chance of your horse ever getting into the grain, a stunt that might cost him his life. (See "founder" in chapter 9.)

Smooth all wooden edges in the barn and avoid using any plywood in areas that your horse can reach, because it splinters easily. Remove all sharp objects that may scratch your horse; countersink all bolts and hammer all nails into place.

Wood within reach of a horse's teeth should be covered with metal, or he will bite, chew, and even swallow it. Trying to save pennies with cheap, poorly made latches, hinges, and other materials may cost you dollars later on in repairs, injuries to your horse, and inconvenience and sorrow to you.

FEED AND WATER EQUIPMENT

Feed and water equipment should be simple, sturdy, and effective. Removable buckets and tubs are easiest to clean and should be suspended by a snap hook on the wall at about the horse's chest height. The water bucket should be located in a front corner of the stall or near the door for easy refilling. Rubber or plastic buckets are better than metal ones, which tend to have sharp edges when bent or dented. Flat-backed ones are made to lie flat against the wall.

Automatic stall waterers may be convenient for large stables; but for the backyard horse owner who has only a horse or two, they are not necessary. With automatic waterers you never know how much your horse is drinking, an important piece of information that can indicate if your horse has a medical problem.

Most horse owners seem to prefer to throw hay on the floor—rather than load it into hayracks or hay nets—this is the more natural way for horses to eat. The argument against this approach is that the hay can get mixed with manure and soiled bedding. But if you clean your stall daily, it should not happen.

In addition to the extra cost, some people think hayracks and hay nets are dangerous. If they aren't high enough, horses have been known to catch their feet in them or bang their knees up against them. Eye injuries are possible from falling dust or small hay stalks from racks or nets that are placed too high.

Grain should be placed in a removable plastic or rubber tub hung at chest height in the opposite front corner of the stall from the water. All feeding and watering containers must be wide enough for a horse to put his head down into it, with room to spare inside.

A salt-block holder made of plastic, rather than metal, should be put on the wall so the horse may have free access to salt. Metal holders, when bent or broken, have sharp edges that can cause serious injuries. The block of salt may also be placed in the feed bucket where the horse can lick it while eating. However, if it crumbles, the horse may get too much salt mixed in with his grain.

Crossties are an important accessory to hold your horse while he's being groomed or tacked up. Put two strong loose-ring eye bolts on either side of your aisle or on opposite stall walls for crossties. An overhang across the front of your barn, at least 6 feet wide, is another area in which you can crosstie your horse.

Crossties should be made of equal length. When stretched across the gap, they should just barely meet in the middle. They should be set at the horse's eye level (approximately 6 feet high) and be made of ½ to ¾-inch cotton rope. They are there to hold the horse, but in an emergency the horse should be able to break away. Two short pieces of sturdy cotton twine connecting the crossties to the eye bolts will allow this to happen.

Two trees are fine for crosstying your horse outside, but they're suitable only in good weather.

You will be thankful for a light in the stall as well as in the aisle if you have to come out to the barn after dark. Run an electric line off your house's current and put it underground so there are no unsightly wires or poles. Make sure it is deep enough so that an errant gardener's shovel doesn't cut into it by accident.

The bulbs should have cages made of wire or wire and glass around them to avoid being broken by a horse tossing his head. An electric outlet in the aisle is both a convenience as well as a necessity when clipping or working with a sick horse.

Aisle lights are best if they are placed down either side rather than in the middle; it's easier to see the sides of the horse as you groom him. All electric wiring should be in metal conduits so rats and mice can't chew on it.

Some of the more convenient items that can be hung from or attached to the outside of the front of the stall—if there is an inside aisle—are a collapsible wooden or metal saddle holder, a hook for halter and lead rope, a box for grooming items, and a name plate.

An automatic fly mister, an optional item to include in your barn, helps keep the flies under control in summer. Another deterrent to flies is to screen off or close windows and doors during the hours they are exposed to direct sunlight. A fire extinguisher is essential.

The tack room and its setup is discussed in chapter 4 and the food-storage area in chapter 5.

FIRE SAFETY

Thirty seconds is all you may have to rescue your horse from a burning barn, so keep your fire department phone number in a conspicuous spot near the telephone—in the house or the barn, if you have one there. Be prepared and put up a smoke alarm and have fire equipment and water at easy reach. Know how to use your extinguisher!

In case of a fire, call the fire department and then get your horse out of the barn. Tie him up away from the blaze so he can't run back into what he thinks is a haven from danger. Use whatever fire equipment and water you have on hand while you're waiting for the firemen to arrive.

MANURE PILE

The manure pile should be in a secluded spot outside the paddock but within wheelbarrow distance of the barn. As mentioned earlier, be sure to locate it according to local zoning restrictions. If you will be having it hauled away, make sure the truck doing the hauling has access to the area.

Manure will attract flies, so the farther away from your horse the pile is, the better. Be sure the pile is also out of sight and smell of residences and downwind from the barn. Manure heaped in a pit or within an enclosed area is tidier than just dumped on the ground.

PADDOCK OR PASTURE

The paddock or pasture should be large enough for your horse to be able to take ten running strides in one direction. If you're short on space, make the paddock long and narrow rather than square to give him an area to stretch his legs.

Level the ground, if possible, and clear the area of protruding rocks, roots, nettles, weeds, and all plants poisonous to horses, such as yews, autumn crocuses, wild cherry, morning glory vine, and nightshade. Call your vet or local agricultural agent for free advice on what is toxic in your area.

If grass is abundant and the horse otherwise well fed, he will usually not sample anything other than the grass menu. Most animals seem to know what plants are poisonous, but years of domestication have removed some horses' "horse sense." Boredom and extreme hunger can also tempt a horse to try nonedible greens, browns, and whatever other color objects he can reach.

The trunks of any trees inside the pasture should be wrapped with chicken wire, or else your horse may strip off their bark, thus girdling and killing them. Fruit trees inside the pasture cannot be sprayed with insecticides that may be toxic to your horse, and fruit that drops on the ground should be picked up so your horse doesn't gorge himself sick.

The larger the pasture, the less chance there is of its becoming a dust bowl or a mudhole. A field used every day by a grazing horse will "die off," and its soil become soured by his droppings. Depending on the size of the pasture and the number of horses grazing there, manure may have to be picked up every couple of days, or at least raked over and spread so the sun's rays can kill worm eggs deposited in it by flies.

For a minimal fee, your county agricultural agent or a specialist at your state agricultural college can recommend a specific grass or grass mix, along with treatment, such as liming, necessary to help maintain your paddock. You will need to send a soil specimen to the agent or specialist.

If there is no shade available in your paddock, leave the stall door open so your horse can get in out of the sun. Tack curtains made from burlap bags at the top of the door so they hang halfway down over the opening. They will keep the stall's interior cooler and larger horseflies out, while your horse and any breezes can still pass through the door.

Many horse owners reverse their turnout schedule during the hot summer months and turn their horse out for the night, leaving him in his stall during the day.

If you have to tie your horse, do so only with the proper equipment: a halter and rope with snap hook. Many horses have never had any experience with ropes, and they injure themselves in unbelievable ways. To avoid unnecessary accidents, be sure to check on your horse frequently. One pony tethered on a hillside slipped and fell with the rope tangled around his neck. Unable to get up because of the steepness of the slope and the tautness of the rope, he eventually strangled to death.

FENCES

Good fences keep horses within their boundaries, preventing danger to your equine pets and damage to your neighbors' property. In the past most horse fences were made of steel or aluminum posts and rails, wooden posts and rails, wooden posts and boards, and wooden posts and heavy-duty wire. Today, there are many more choices.

Vinyl rails with wood posts, PVC (polyvinyl chloride) post and rail, metal rail fencing, wire mesh fencing, and electric fencing are types of high-tech fencing that use vinyls, plastics, and new steel products. These more modern fences were created to eliminate the high cost of maintaining older fences and to cut down on the injuries many horses received from the more traditional enclosures.

However, there are pros and cons to both the traditional and the high-tech fencing. Cost and looks are the initial concerns and must be compared with maintenance and safety.

Split-rail fencing or posts and boards were always the most popular. But wood posts must be creosoted or pressure-treated before being put into the ground to protect them from moisture and eventual rotting, and the maintenance of this fencing over the years is very time consuming. You can save some money on posts, however, by using sturdy trees growing along the edge of the paddock.

Good fences keep horses within their boundaries.

Boards should be fastened to the inside of the posts; this construction is not as attractive from the outside but is much sturdier. Boards that are painted rather than allowed to weather naturally will have to be repainted regularly.

Horses tend to chew and lean on fences, so to discourage this practice and to preserve your fences, add a single strand of electric wire across the top toward the inside of the fence. Any contact with the activated wire will give your horse a jolt—not a dangerous one—that will remind him to keep his distance. Your neighbors won't like the shock either, so install signs on the fence to warn them of its existence.

If you plan to use only an electric strand without a fence to contain your horse, place the wire chest-high and teach the animal to respect it. Otherwise, when you turn your pet loose, he may charge through the wire and not even feel the shock. Put a halter and a long lead rope on the horse and allow him to graze up to one of the strands. After touching it at each side of the pasture or paddock, your pet will keep a safe distance.

Wire is the least expensive adequate fencing available. Avoid barbed wire, which can do serious injury to a horse if he gets tangled up in it, and agricultural wire, which is cheap but has a weak top and large openings. Instead, use a woven wire fencing with small mesh so your horse can't catch his foot in it. A wooden board across the top will keep the wire from sagging.

Your choice of fencing will depend on the type of terrain your pasture is located on, how much time you plan to spend maintaining the fence, how important aesthetics are, what sort of horse or horses you have (tricky little ponies or larger spirited horses may require very different fencing), and how much money you wish to spend on fencing!

Before making your decision, drive around and look at various fences, either around other horse pastures or at fence dealers. Try to talk to other horse owners who have different kinds of fencing and ask how they like them.

Gates in the fencing should be at least 8 feet wide, and even wider if you are planning to drive a tractor or truck through them. They should be solid with sturdy, horseproof hardware. Openings in electric fencing are made with large hooks that snap onto a loop in the wire. Their handles contain a spring for easy latching and unlatching, and are insulated so people don't get a shock when touching them. Gates in fencing usually swing in and out.

PLAY EQUIPMENT

Older, docile horses may not need any diversions to keep them occupied, but a young, spirited animal will welcome the chance to play.

A horse loves to roll and scratch his back, especially in the spring when he is shedding his itchy, dry winter coat. A load of sand dumped in a convenient spot in the paddock will be a welcome addition. Sand is a lot cleaner than mud and manure, and it will even help to groom your horse's coat as you brush it out later.

A plastic gallon-size milk container hanging from the stall's ceiling at head height can be fun for your horse to poke at or butt. A handful of gravel placed inside will add to the fun, and if the container is hung at his withers' height your horse may enjoy walking under it to bounce it off his back.

A soccerball or basketball in the paddock can be kicked or pushed from one side to the other. At the ball's slightest movement, your horse will use up excess energy rearing in mock terror or kicking up his heels and charging about— rather than getting into mischief with the fences or barn.

3

Pinto, Paint, or Palomino?

Buying the right horse for your family requires a great deal of thought before you even start looking. Decide, first of all, on your price range (how much you can afford to spend), who's going to ride the horse, and what you want to do with him. Enlist the help of a knowledgeable horse person to aid you in making some of these decisions—either a horse-owning friend, your child's riding instructor, or a veterinarian specializing in equines.

WHAT BREED?

Horse breeds used to be fairly easy to list, but today there are over seventy-five different breed organizations in the United States. Some are duplicates or rival associations of the same breed, but, nevertheless, there are more breeds than ever from which to choose. Most of these "new" breeds have been imported from Europe, such as the Hanoverian and the Oldenburg.

Any one of the Light Horse breeds (different from the heavy draft horses used for hauling) are excellent choices, depending on your use. But a purebred—an Arabian, a Morgan, thoroughbred, or Quarter Horse—is going to be more expensive than a crossbred or just a plain horse (referred to as "grade").

Thoroughbreds are often too "hot" or nervous and spirited for a family or a novice rider. They may also be more sensitive and require extra, specialized care and facilities.

What you plan on doing with your horse will determine what breed or type you want. Will your new horse be used primarily for pleasure riding, to teach a youngster to ride, or to compete in dressage shows? Ask your child's riding instructor what type of horse you should buy to match the child's riding ability.

Crossbreds make excellent backyard horses, but a horse with some thoroughbred in him will be better for jumping, while one with Quarter Horse in his background should do well at gymkhana events, such as barrel racing.

There are more Quarter Horses than any other breed in this country. A Quarter Horse or a horse with some Quarter Horse breeding is a good, sturdy pet that adapts well to a backyard and meets most demands made by the average rider. However, the same things can be said about numerous other breeds, too.

Arabian horse owners claim that horses with Arabian in them are excellent for children because of their smaller size and superior intelligence, but Arabians have been known to be flighty and excitable.

Tennessee Walking Horse fans say these horses are good backyard horses for novice owners because they are easy to learn to ride. They are noted for their smooth running walk that you can just sit to, but this smooth riding gait also makes them unsuitable for a child who wants to show and jump in regular horse shows. And if you are planning to trail ride with friends on horses of other breeds, the gaits are sometimes not compatible. The running walk is too fast for the walk of other horses and too slow for their trot.

Morgans are supposed to be a sturdy, steady horse. However, there has been so much breeding "for show" that many of the qualities that the Morgans were originally noted for have been lost.

Saddlebreds are usually much too high-strung to be a good backyard horse. This is true of any of the breeds whose individuals have been bred, raised, and trained as show horses, such as Arabians and Tennessee Walkers. They are pretty and flashy, with high-stepping gaits, but this isn't what you are looking for when it comes to trail riding with your family.

Some of the breeds now being seen in dressage shows and Grand Prix jumping contests—Hanoverians, Holsteiners, Trakhaners, Oldenburgs, Dutch and Swedish Warmbloods—are much too expensive for the average family to buy for their backyard. They are a combination of a draft horse (coldblood) and, usually, a thoroughbred (hotblood) making them a warmblood. Another strike against them as a children's mount is their size. Their draft horse background make them considerably taller and heavier than the average horse—usually well over 16 hands. (See the discussion on size in this chapter.)

A pony may be your logical choice if your only rider is to be a small child. They are cute and fuzzy with a strong sense of self-preservation, and, while cunning and mischievous, they have been used to teach the children in an entire family to ride before being passed on to the local Pony Club and its novice riders.

There are many different breeds of ponies from which to choose, ranging from the tiny Shetland to the larger Welsh and Connemara ponies. Their suitability depends on the size of your child—a small pony (under 12 hands) for a small child, a larger pony (between 12 and 14.2 hands) for a larger child. (Size is covered later in this chapter.)

The "Heinz 57" variety of horse or pony often exhibits the best of the many breeds in his background and will do well in your backyard. In fact, some of our best equine athletes and show horses have been of unknown parentage.

Many horse lovers have a favorite breed or two and think they produce the perfect horse, but there are good and bad individuals in every breed. Judge the horse you're thinking of buying as an individual, not just by his particular breed. Follow the criteria listed below and you will end up with a good example of what you should be looking for in a backyard horse.

WHAT PRICE?

There are no set prices on horses, and whatever the market will bear plays an important part in "the bottom line." Circumstances, too, are a determining factor. The seller may need stall space because his new horse is arriving any day and so will sell you his old horse cheap. But if you, the buyer, fall in love with a horse and just have to have him no matter what, you may well pay more than the horse is actually worth.

Value is usually based on a horse's age, size, soundness,

conformation, temperament, manners, schooling, breeding, and athletic ability. It is rare for a horse to have the best of all these qualities, so you will have to decide which are most important to you and then sacrifice the others.

A good price for a crossbred or grade horse may be only a few hundred dollars. Sometimes you can even find for free an older mare or gelding that needs a good home and is just perfect for your family and their needs. An unbroken Shetland pony may sell at a local livestock auction for as little as $10, while purebreds can run into the hundreds of thousands of dollars.

However, beware of bargains. They are often someone else's throwaways and may not be right for your family at all, possibly even dangerous. An inexpensive thoroughbred off the track may be cheap because he has had little training and is probably very excitable or "hot." Another competitor, such as a retired barrel racer, may be for sale at a low price because his legs are in bad shape after years of sharp turns in competitions.

WHAT SIZE?

A pony might be the best choice if the new pet is to be ridden only by a small child. But if all the family members plan on riding, a small, sturdy horse is the best size. A good average height is between 14.2 and 15.2 hands. (A hand is 4 inches, the unit of measurement used in telling horses' and ponies' height. A horse that is 15.2 hands measures 62 inches from the ground to the point of his withers.) The dividing line between horses and ponies is 14.2 hands. Under this height, the animal is a pony; over, it is considered a horse.

If your youngster is a growing teenager, do not choose a

If you have a growing teenager, do not choose a horse or pony that is just the right size for her now, because in a year's time she may outgrow the horse.

horse or pony that is just the right size for her now, because in a year it may look as if her feet are dragging on the ground. A horse that is much too big is not right either, for your child will probably have trouble saddling and bridling him, brushing his back and head, and even mounting him. In addition, more height in a horse usually means more money.

A horse that is too big will be a problem to saddle, bridle, clean, and mount.

A horse is the right size for your child when her knees hit the widest part of the horse's barrel as she sits on his back.

WHAT SEX?

The gender of your pet-to-be is another important consideration. Many young people dream wistfully of a fiery spirited stallion carrying them swiftly over hill and dale, but such a horse is really quite impractical as a family pet. Of course, we've all heard of the gentle stallions who give pony rides to the grandchildren in the family without saddle or bridle, shuffling docilely along like ancient plugs, but such individuals are few and far between.

Stallions are usually much too powerful and unruly for any but the most skilled of equestrians and can be dangerous to riders and other horses if aroused by a mare in season. Many stables won't even allow stallions to be boarded in their establishments.

Mares are easier to manage than stallions and make good, reliable mounts, depending on the individual, except when in season. Then they may be a little cranky and temperamental. A mare will usually be in season for four to six days, with intervals between heat periods ranging from ten to thirty-seven days.

The best choice for a backyard horse is a gelding (a castrated male). Most colts are gelded, so there are many available. They can never be used for breeding, so they are often cheaper than a mare or stallion of equal ability, and since they have no desire for the opposite sex, they are usually more even-tempered and predictable. (As geldings are the most popular for beginners, the pronoun *he* is used in this book when talking about your horse.)

WHAT AGE?

The age of a horse is not to be overlooked, but for a backyard horse you have quite a wide range of years from which to choose.

The typical riding horse is between five and twenty years old. Any horse younger than five will probably be too green and too spirited for the average family. A horse's life span is between twenty and thirty years, so any animal over twenty is considered a senior citizen. Ponies, however, have a longer life span and can live past thirty if taken care of properly.

Don't try to predict a horse's soundness by his age. Some horses are old at ten while others over twenty are still safe, healthy mounts. Not all older horses are necessarily gentle and slow, either. Age does mellow most, but it is not an infallible rule. Your vet can tell you a horse's age and whether he is sound during his pre-vet exam. (See How to Buy a Horse, later in this chapter.)

Older horses tend to be smarter and know all the tricks, but usually they also have more common sense than a younger animal. A horse between eight and fourteen is of a good intermediate age, not too old or too young.

WHAT COLOR?

Color should be the least important of your concerns. Whether your pet is chestnut, roan, or bay, pinto, paint, or palomino, you should be satisfied, as long as he fits your other criteria.

The only real difference in color is that some need a little extra care to stay looking nice. Grays, paints, and Appaloosas are harder to keep clean because manure and mud stains show up more. You also have to be careful with grays because they are apt to get melanomas (skin cancer tumors) when left out in the sun. They and any other horses with a lot of white on them can get sunburned, too. (It is not unusual to see a pink, peeling nose under the white on a blaze-faced horse.)

A black horse may be as shiny as a piece of coal, but if left out in the hot, bright sun, his coat will soon fade to a rusty brown.

WHAT TEMPERAMENT?

The two most important requirements for a backyard horse are soundness and gentleness: soundness, or good health, so that you can ride whenever you wish, and—just as important—gentleness, so you do not have to worry that you or your family or neighborhood children will be thrown or kicked.

A spirited horse versus a docile horse is another way of looking at equine temperament, but the ideal animal will have a little of each. No one wants a horse that mopes along as if it were half dead, head hanging to the ground, and its rider kicking with every step to keep it going. But, on the other hand, no one wants to see children on an out-of-control beast that races back to the barn whenever it feels like it or spooks and spins at every little rustle in the bushes.

A reliable horse with a good disposition and a sensible nature is a joy to work around and to ride. Never buy a horse that you fear, no matter how beautiful he is, because his behavior will get worse as he senses your fear. He will begin to bully and take advantage of you, and you will become more afraid of him. The result could be an unnecessary accident.

Look for a horse that has good ground manners, one that doesn't crowd, bite, or kick, but stands quietly. He should pick up his feet when you want to clean them. A little handling while looking him over the first time can indicate these things.

You want a horse that loads easily onto a trailer. A horse that doesn't mind clippers or being wormed—and one that is sensible on the trails when encountering barking dogs, overflowing garbage cans, and passing cars—is definitely an asset. However, unless you can take the horse on a trial period, you won't know these things until you have him at home.

WHERE TO BUY A HORSE?

There are many places to find a horse: through advertisements in your local paper or tack shop bulletin board, from a veterinarian or farrier, or by word-of-mouth from horsey friends.

You may even find your ideal pet at the stable where you or your children have been taking riding lessons, although the owner may be reluctant to sell any horses from his or her string of reliable mounts.

Buy a horse only from a dealer who is reputable and well recommended by other horse owners who have done business with him. Ask for references from the dealer, and ask other horse people you know what they have heard about him. Satisfied customers are a dealer's best advertisement, so you can expect fair treatment if a dealer has a good reputation.

Your local equine veterinarian or farrier may know of a family horse for sale. Keep in mind that not all veterinarians treat horses. Some are small-animal practitioners only. Look for those whose specialty is horses; because of their calls on nearby barns, they will know what's going on within the local horse community.

Caution is advised if you plan to attend a horse auction that advertises 100 Head of Fresh Horses just in from the West. Horses may seem to be cheaper here than those from a private dealer, but it takes a real expert and a lot of luck to strike a good bargain at an auction. These "Western broomtails" are usually problem horses that no one else in the area wants, or else they've been shipped in from another auction. Remember, a winning bid means that the horse is yours—there is no trial period or return privilege if you are not satisfied.

Tranquilizing a wild pony or pepping up an exhausted, worn-out horse with hormones is illegal, but it's also hard to detect at auctions because you have little chance to really examine these animals. Some sellers have even been known to shoot a horse's legs with novocaine to eliminate soreness, or shoe them in ways to hide poor gaits, sore feet, and lameness, or even feed them small quantities of arsenic, which adds almost instant weight to any "bag of bones." Without the arsenic—eventually poisonous and addictive—pounds disappear, and the newly acquired horse soon returns to his former skeletal condition.

Your local SPCA may have a horse or a pony for you at a very reasonable price. The SPCA often picks up cruelty cases or receives animals donated by people who cannot afford to keep them anymore but want them to get a good home. Before the SPCA will allow you to adopt a horse, it will inspect your facilities, make sure you know how to care for a horse, and check periodically to see that you are keeping the horse in good condition.

Adopting a wild mustang may be a noble thought, but these horses are seldom, if ever, an ideal beginner's horse.

Summer camps and seasonal riding academies may offer you a horse for ten months of the year if you will pay for his feed and board. They use the horse only during the camping season and look for a home for him the rest of the year to help defray the cost of year-round care. These horses are usually well-trained, quiet mounts for novice riders.

Another possibility is to care for a horse for a friend or neighbor who is leaving for a long vacation or going away to college. Riding privileges are yours in return.

Advertisements in bigger newspapers and nationally distributed magazines usually cost too much to justify advertising a "backyard horse."

HOW TO BUY A HORSE

There are no black-and-white guidelines to follow when buying a horse, so when you are planning to make an actual purchase, be sure to take along a veterinarian and, as stated earlier in this chapter, another knowledgeable person to examine the horse.

"Know what you know and know what you don't know" sounds like gibberish, but it makes sense. You may be able to see whether a horse is nice-looking or not, but will you be able to tell how old he is and how good his gaits and conformation are? Can you tell whether he is sound and physically able to do what you want—jump, turn quickly, run fast, or participate in fairly long pleasure rides without becoming exhausted or sore?

A veterinarian will be able to give you an overall picture of the horse's general health during a presale vet exam. He will check the horse's age (accurate up to age ten and within two to four years after that) by looking at his teeth.

After carefully checking the horse's eyes, the vet will start at the neck and go all over the body, legs, and feet, looking for faulty conformation, such as a too narrow chest, parrot mouth, or weak pasterns, that might cause future disabilities. (See page 49.)

Blood or urine samples can be taken to detect any drugs,

and a Coggins test detects equine infectious anemia. The veterinarian will also ask the owner about the horse's medical history and find out what shots and worming have been administered, so that you will know what has to be done as the new owner. The vet will check the horse's heart, lungs, and wind after the animal has been ridden.

What a veterinarian cannot do is guarantee a horse completely. A tumor of the internal organs, bone chips, and other problems that may show up only after a period of extensive work or as the horse ages cannot be spotted.

A veterinarian is not supposed to comment on the horse's training, suitability for the buyer, conformation, or disposition other than what would affect the horse's ability to do the job the buyer wishes him to do. (These are things a knowledgeable friend will help you with.) He will question you about your plans for the horse to determine if a minor defect might interfere with them. What may impede a jumper or barrel racer may cause no problems for a trail rider or pleasure class competitor.

A trial period of a week or two is given by many sellers, sometimes for an extra fee. Try to get the horse for at least three days to make sure any drugs are out of his system and to see how he behaves when worked around. If this trial period is impossible, watch the horse being ridden. Then let your child try riding him, too, to determine the horse's suitability for her. If your child is a beginner, let your knowledgeable friend ride the horse for you, trying out all the horse's gaits and testing to see whether he minds traffic and stands for dismounting and mounting.

Your expert friend will watch the horse move when being ridden by the seller and will watch the horse's reactions when being handled. He will approach the horse slowly,

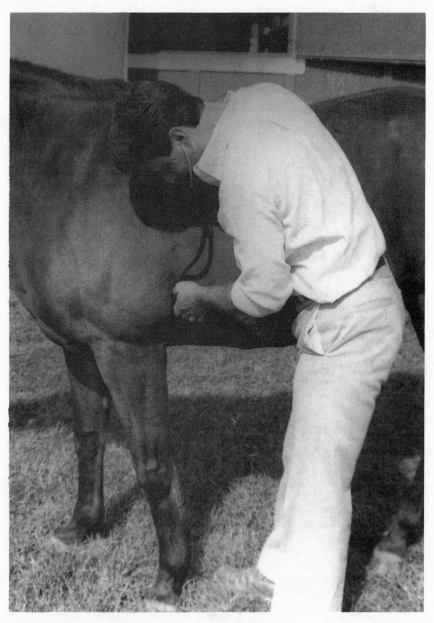

A presale vet exam is very important before buying a horse.

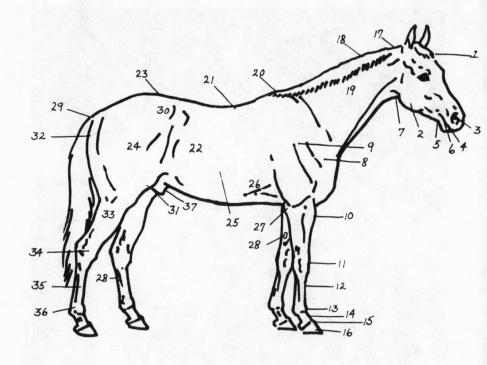

Points of the Horse

1. Forehead	13. Fetlock	26. Heart Girth
2. Cheek	14. Pastern	27. Elbow
3. Nostril	15. Coronet Band	28. Chestnut
4. Lips	16. Hoof	29. Dock or Root of
5. Chin Groove	17. Poll	Tail
6. Bars of Jaw	18. Crest	30. Point of Hip
7. Throttle	19. Neck	31. Stifle
8. Point of	20. Withers	32. Point of Rump
Shoulder	21. Back	33. Gaskin
9. Shoulder	22. Flank	34. Hock
10. Forearm	23. Croup	35. Rear Cannon
11. Knee	24. Loins	36. Rear Fetlock
12. Cannon	25. Barrel	37. Sheath

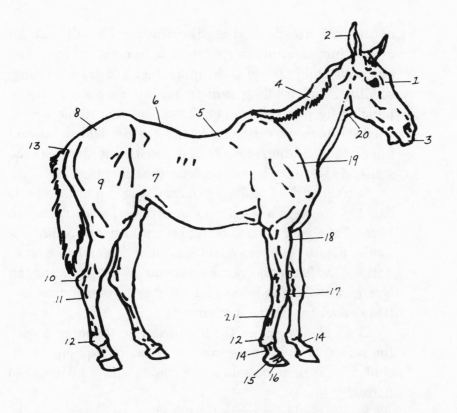

Conformation Faults

1. Small Pig Eye
2. Mule Ears
3. Parrot Mouth
4. Ewe Neck
5. Sway Back
6. Roach
7. Light Waist
8. Goose Rump
9. Weak Quarter
10. Capped Hock
11. Sickle Hocks
12. Lumpy Fetlock
13. Tail Attached Too Low
14. Weak Pasterns
15. Club Foot
16. Founder Rings
17. Over at Knee
18. Weak Forearms
19. Straight Shoulder
20. Thick Gullet
21. Bowed Tendon

noting both friendly and hostile behavior. He will walk all around him carefully to see whether he bites or kicks. You and your child should pick up his feet and try grooming, saddling, and bridling him to see his reaction to being handled by a novice. Other "tests" might include seeing whether the horse can be caught easily in a field and checking on the condition of his stall to see whether he kicks the walls, chews, or cribs on the door. (See chapter 7.)

Don't buy the first horse you try (you can always come back). A horse is a long-term investment, so don't buy in haste. Take your time and test several. Anyone selling reliable, healthy horses should not mind a complete examination. Evaluate the horse's present owner by watching how he handles the horse and whether he seems conscientious about caring for the horse.

Don't always accept the first price. Try to bargain with the seller. Is the horse's tack or grooming equipment included, or is he to be sold as he stands with a tattered old halter?

Price should be partially based on the horse's skills. Does he back easily, stand without fidgeting, take both leads when cantering? If Western trained, does he neck-rein? Do you have to kick him constantly to keep him moving? Does he respond easily to the reins or almost jerk you out of the saddle? These are all things you can correct or teach, but they are also good points you can haggle over to bring the asking price down.

Aim for perfection in your selection and then decide what you can do without. A skinny, unkempt animal with a low price tag may, with care, develop into a nice riding horse for you and your family. A ewe neck (see page 49) is hardly as bad a defect as cracked heels or navicular changes in the feet. (See chapter 9.)

Perfection costs money, but don't compromise on good manners in and out of the stall, soundness, or gentleness. A horse with quality is always easier to resell if and when you go on to a more advanced horse.

When you purchase the horse, be sure you receive from the seller a written and dated warranty of the terms: guarantees of the horse's age, its soundness in wind and limb, freedom from vices like kicking and biting, and suitability for your purpose. The contract should also state the price, whether tack and transportation are included, whether the seller holds clear title to the horse, and whether the horse can be returned if the above written description is not accurate. (See below.)

Buying a horse is a personal matter. Be sure to pick one that you like and trust.

Sample Warranty

I, _____ , agree to sell _____ , my ten-year-old Quarter Horse cross to _____ for $900. A halter and lead rope are included in the sale. Buyer agrees to pay for transporting the horse to his barn.

A down payment of $100 is due upon signature of this warranty, and the remainder ($800) is due the day the horse is picked up.

I guarantee that _____ is an experienced, healthy trail horse with no known vices. He should be a perfect family riding horse. I will return the full price of $900 if during the next two weeks he is proven otherwise and returned.

_____ Signature (Seller)

_____ Signature (Buyer)

_____ Date

4

Snaffle to Saddle

Tack is the horseman's term for all equipment put on a horse: saddle, bridle, halter, and so on. Before choosing your tack, decide first whether you are going to ride English or Western style. There are different sets of tack, with many variations, for each style. You should not try to mix and match the two kinds of tack but should acquire either one or the other.

If you have been taking riding lessons, you will probably want to continue in the style that you have been learning. But if you have experience in both English and Western, you will then have to decide what to do with your horse in the future. Speed events, such as barrel races, are much easier to perform with Western gear, but an English hunt saddle is made for jumping. However, everyday riding for pleasure is done with either Western or English tack.

WESTERN TACK

The Western Saddle

The Western saddle was once an intricate part of the Old West. Today's models, often more elaborate than those of the past, are available in three basic frames for: (1) most Quarter Horses, (2) Arabians, and (3) horses of any breed with higher withers.

When you buy Western saddles, stirrups and girths are included, but it is a good idea to get a spare girth. Saddles range in price from a couple of hundred dollars to several thousand dollars for handmade, jewel-encrusted, silver-studded show saddles. The average saddle costs between $500 and $700 although you can find some on sale for under $500.

A Blanket or Pad

A blanket or pad should be used under a Western saddle to give added protection to the horse's back. The most popular are the handwoven, all-wool Navaho saddle pads, which start at $50 and go up to over $80. There are also attractive but thin acrylic-blend blankets, which may be purchased for under $5, but these give little protection to your horse's back. Pads are often cut to the outline of the saddle and may have felt centers and fleece lining for extra comfort for the horse. Buy two, especially if you live in a warm climate, so you will always have a dry one to use.

The Western Bridle

The Western bridle, like its English counterpart, has a bit, a crownpiece, a throatlatch, a browband, and a noseband,

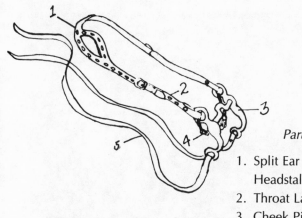

Parts of the Western Bridle

1. Split Ear Headstall
2. Throat Latch
3. Cheek Piece
4. Grazing Bit
5. Curb Chain
6. Reins

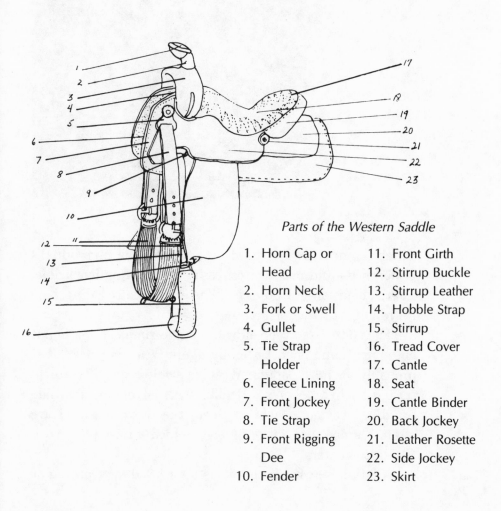

Parts of the Western Saddle

1. Horn Cap or Head
2. Horn Neck
3. Fork or Swell
4. Gullet
5. Tie Strap Holder
6. Fleece Lining
7. Front Jockey
8. Tie Strap
9. Front Rigging Dee
10. Fender
11. Front Girth
12. Stirrup Buckle
13. Stirrup Leather
14. Hobble Strap
15. Stirrup
16. Tread Cover
17. Cantle
18. Seat
19. Cantle Binder
20. Back Jockey
21. Leather Rosette
22. Side Jockey
23. Skirt

A properly attired Western-tacked horse.

which is not always used—it's up to the individual's preference—and called a cavesson on the English bridle. There are different bridles for Western pleasure riding, barrel racing, cutting, or training.

The split-eared type of bridle is the simplest one to put on, is neat, and is still used by many Western riders. It is probably the most popular Western bridle used on Western-tacked backyard horses. Bridles with silver and rawhide braiding are more fashionable in the show ring and are often teamed up with silver-trimmed browbands with V-shaped centers.

A bosal, which has no bit, is often used for training or

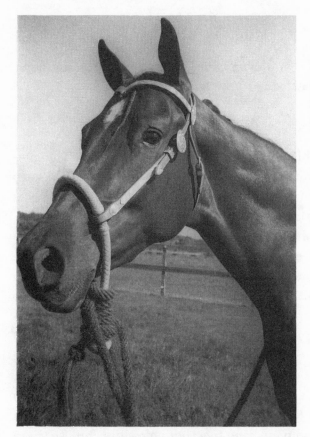

A bosel, which has no bit, is often used for training or schooling young horses.

schooling young horses. It has reins that are knotted under the horse's jaw and a headstall with a plaited rawhide or rope noseband.

The mechanical hackamore, which also has no bit, is hinged to put pressure on the nose and under the jaw. It doesn't give instant and precise control, and is rarely used for reining or pleasure. But it is ideal for barrel racing and roping, where fast starts and sudden stops are needed.

Nylon bridles in a variety of colors are cheaper than leather bridles. Many Western riders like the different colors and the fact that nylon needs very little care. However, nylon is abrasive and if you are not careful it can rub the hair off a horse and even cause sores if not fitted properly and checked periodically.

The Western Bit

The Western bit also has a number of variations. The gentlest is a shank snaffle, a flexible mouthpiece with a curb chain and shanks for control. But remember that a bit is only as gentle as the hands of the rider.

Stronger bits are the grazing bit and the curb. They are similar, but the grazing bit's shanks curve back out of the way so the horse can graze with the bit in his mouth—an annoying habit that you should never allow your horse to acquire. They may each have a port, or hump, on the mouthpiece (the wider and more shallow ports are the mildest) and shanks or cheeks that vary in length from 6 to 9 inches.

The longer the shanks are, the more severe the bit is in the horse's mouth. The most severe is a spade bit—never to be used by a beginner. A roping bit has its two shanks curving down and meeting together below the chin, so there is less chance of the rope getting caught in it.

Bits can be chrome- or nickel-plated, copper coated, made of hard rubber or stainless steel. Stainless steel bits are the most durable, and are recommended for backyard horses. Most bits range in price from $25 to $75.

Reins

Reins come in various widths, so you can choose the one that best fits your hands. They may be of leather, rope, or horsehair—braided or flat. Except for those on a roping bridle, which are of one piece, Western reins are usually long and split in the middle. The average range in price is from $12 to $30.

ENGLISH TACK

There are three basic types of English saddles: the forward seat or hunt saddle for jumping, the park saddle for saddle-seat riding, and the dressage saddle. In these categories are endurance saddles, polo saddles, eventing saddles, and all-purpose saddles, most of which have various options, such as knee rolls, padded suede flaps, narrow to extra-wide tree widths, long billets, and cutback heads.

The hunt seat is the most popular style among English riders. It ranges from about $200 for one made in Argentina to over $2,000 for the best European models. The average hunt saddle costs from $400 to $800.

Unlike Western fittings, stirrups (leathers and irons) and girth usually do not come with the English saddle. You must buy them separately.

Stirrups

Stirrups are either nickel- or chrome-plated, or of stainless steel. The "never rust" ones are the most practical, and stainless steel the hardest. Make sure the stirrup fits your child's foot. The widest part of the foot should fit into it with an inch to spare on each side.

Also available are safety stirrups and offset stirrups. Safety stirrups have a heavy rubber band on one side of the stirrup so that if the rider falls and her foot is caught, the band will unhook, releasing the foot. Safety stirrups should always be used on bareback pads where stirrups are attached to metal dees rather than a saddle's safety bar.

Offset stirrups have the slot for the leather off center (to the right on a right-hand iron). This throws the knee in, and the sloping footrest keeps the heel down. Some people feel that this stirrup helps their position during a show.

Stirrups range from $15 to $40, depending on their size and quality. Rubber treads, which keep the foot from slipping back and forth, are often included, but if they are not, buy a pair for a couple of dollars.

Leathers

Leathers, which attach the stirrups to the saddle, range in price from $27 to $45 for a children's size and up to $90 for those made in Germany of top quality leather.

Girths

Girths are available in leather, vinyl, webbing, cord, mohair, or nylon. They may also be shaped at the horse's elbows to prevent chafing. The cord and mohair girths are washable. They allow air to circulate through them and so are practical for a very hot day or on muddy trails. Have two: a mohair one and another of leather for everyday use and showing.

The average girth costs from about $15 to $50, but the price can go much higher for English girths of the finest leather.

Pads

Pads under English saddles help to protect both the horse's back and the underside of the saddle. (A horse's sweat will rot the leather in time.) These pads can be made of synthetic sheepskin—or Equi-Fleece, which is mothproof and mildewproof and can be thrown into the washer—real sheepskin, cotton, felt, quilted flannel, and wool. Double-faced pads are available for supersensitive backs.

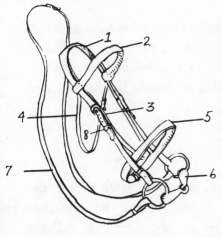

Parts of the English Bridle

1. Crownpiece or Headstall
2. Brow Band
3. Cheek Piece
4. Throat Latch
5. Cavesson
6. Snaffle Bit
7. Reins
8. Keepers

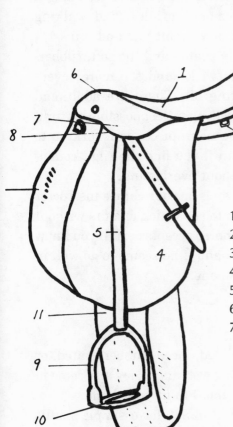

Parts of the English Saddle

1. Seat
2. Cantle
3. Panel
4. Flap
5. Stirrup Leather
6. Pommel
7. Skirt
8. Stirrup Bar
9. Stirrup Iron
10. Tread of Stirrup Iron
11. Girth
12. Knee Roll
13. Dee Rings

Pads start at just under $30 for those of cotton and go up to $60 for the Equi-Fleece pads. They can be rectangular or contoured to follow your saddle's shape—both are popular. Pads with foam inserts are also available to prevent sore backs.

English Bridles and Bits

English bridles and bits, and what combination to buy, depend on what the horse is being used for and the education of both horse and rider. There are show bridles, Pelham bridles, snaffle bridles, Weymouth bridles, and walking horse bridles that come with or without bits and reins.

Bits range from the gentle snaffle and the soft, rubbermouth Pelham to the Kimberwicke and the more severe high port brace cheek walking bit. There are additional variations among the bits. Try the gentlest possible bit first, such as a snaffle with a thick mouthpiece, and work up to stronger ones, if necessary, until you find the right combination for controllability without overbitting.

Borrow some bits from friends or your child's instructor before you buy one. Try them to see which one fits without pinching and which one your horse accepts best. If you know which bit he has been using—and if he seems to go well in it—you can just buy the same one.

Reins

Reins can be all leather (braided, laced, rubber coated, or plain), of linen cord, or of strong webbing. They also come in various widths (¼ inch to ⅞ inch) to fit your hand.

English bridles start at $28 to $30 for a simple snaffle bridle and go up to a few hundred dollars for a double bridle. The average bridle costs from $50 to $100. Bits average in price from $12 to $35. Reins start at $10 and go up to over $100, the average costing between $20 and $50.

TACK ACCESSORIES

There are a number of other pieces of equipment that you will need, but do not be pressured into buying everything that catches your youngster's eye. Many inexperienced horse owners go overboard and never use half of what they buy, filling a trunk with odds and ends that mildew or rust, some still in their original wrappings.

The more equipment you put on your horse (running martingales, side reins, fancy bits, etc.), the more "crutches" you are using to ride him. A lightweight bridle and simple snaffle bit suffice for a competent rider and a well-mannered horse.

Although a breastplate, martingale, saddlebags, and spurs may appeal to your youngster, they may not really be necessary. Breastplates are for horses with heavy or undefined withers to keep their saddles in place during a strenuous ride or when making quick turns.

Martingales or tie-downs (Western terminology) keep a horse's head down. Be sure if you use one that it is not too tight and does not hinder your horse's balance. Your child's instructor should be able to tell you if one is necessary and what kind to use.

Saddlebags and spurs are useful items, too, but if you have no use for the bags and your horse has no need of the spurs, they are a waste of money. Spurs are for dead-sided horses who ignore the drumming heels of their riders and plod merrily along at their own pace—*slow!* However, spurs

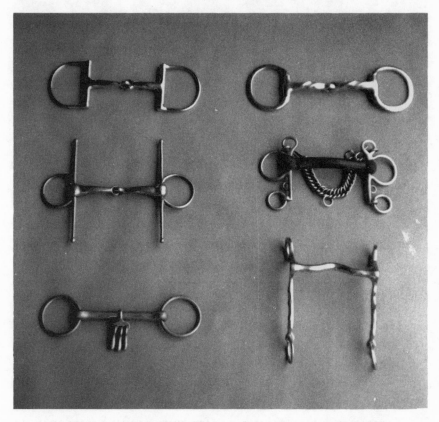

Shown above are both English and Western bits. Clockwise from top left, they are: D-ring snaffle, twisted egg butt snaffle, rubbed-mouthed Pelham, common Western bit, bar-mouth breaking bit with keys, and full cheek snaffle.

on uneducated feet can be cruel to the horse and dangerous to the rider.

If you or your child do wear spurs, remove them when you are working on the ground so they don't trip you.

A crop, bat, whip, or quirt should be used with discretion, and these should rarely be in the hands of a beginner.

Halters and Lead Ropes

Halters and lead ropes are essential pieces of tack to be included in your barn. Depending on your horse, the climate you live in, and how your horse will be used, you may also want to add a longeing line, blankets, and a sheet or cooler to your shopping list.

Halters are made of leather, nylon, or braided cotton. Leather and nylon halters are most popular, and each has its pros and cons. Leather will break if yanked hard enough (which most horsemen feel is a plus in certain emergencies, such as when a horse catches his hoof in the halter while scratching his cheek). If wide enough, leather is less likely than nylon to chafe your horse's skin and rub off his hair—another plus.

Nylon needs little care but will not break, so if a horse wearing one catches a foot in it he may fall over and break a leg or his neck. If he gets the halter caught on something—such as a tree, bush, or even the fence or perhaps the hook that holds the water bucket in his stall—and then panics, he may injure and even strangle himself while trying to get free. However, some nylon halters have a breakable crownpiece of leather to prevent such an accident.

Nylon halters are less expensive and last longer, but they are more apt to rub and even cut your horse. Halters cost about $5 for nylon and up to $50 for a raised, braided halter of the finest leather. Have at least two, one as a spare when the other is mislaid or being repaired.

Confused? Wondering how you'll ever be able to choose the right tack? Don't worry; your child's riding instructor and/or your local tack store owner can decipher some of the above jargon and help you with your decision.

FITTING THE TACK

The most important point to remember when buying tack for the new horse is that it should fit him without the use of any homemade devices such as extra blankets or pads to keep the saddle's pommel from pressing into his withers or spine.

Halters and bridles are sized for horses, cobs (small horses), and ponies; and they have adjustable headstalls for large and small heads. Bits come in various sizes (4½ inches for ponies to 5½ inches for horses), and saddles come with cut-back pommels for horses with high withers.

Unlike the other pieces of tack, the saddle should fit the rider as well as the horse. Hunt saddles come in several seat sizes, from 15 inches for children to 19 inches for adults. Equitation (flat) saddles go up to 21 inches, and Western saddles have seat sizes of 13, 14, 15, and 16 inches. Your tack shop owner or riding instructor are best able to measure and fit your child and the horse.

BUYING TACK

Tack is available in various qualities. The cheaper pieces of gear may be bought for less money initially, but eventually you may end up spending more money on repairs and replacements. Better care must be taken of cheaper tack to maintain it.

The most expensive tack is for those who can afford the very best in leather, craftsmanship, and sometimes the snob appeal of sporting the brand name of a well-known European saddlemaker.

Buy the best quality of medium-priced tack that you can

afford from a reputable dealer. With proper care by your child, the equipment will last for many years.

If you cannot afford to buy a new quality saddle (your most expensive item), check a reliable tack shop for trade-ins. The store may have just what you want in your youngster's size at a more reasonable price and already broken in. Be sure the tree (the frame of the saddle) is sound and the stitching intact.

Buying used tack is also a good idea for someone with a first horse who has not completely decided on a riding style and may switch from English to Western, or vice versa.

CLEANING TACK

Most horse owners take great pride in riding with clean tack. More important is the fact that clean, regularly checked bridles, reins, stirrup leathers, and girths may actually save the rider from a nasty fall.

Your son or daughter may spend hours grooming the new horse, but cleaning tack is definitely not as much fun. In fact, it turns into a chore very quickly. You should help your youngsters learn the proper way to clean tack right from the beginning, and they will be more apt to do it on a regular basis themselves.

Before being used, new tack should be scrubbed with a neutral pH soap such as Ivory, Castile, or Murphy's Oil Soap—not detergent. Use a stiff brush or plastic Tuffy, but only on the unfinished side of leather. Next rub Lexol or neat's-foot oil into the leather, using your fingers or a sponge. Do not oil the saddle's seat and outside flaps, where it would come off on clothing. Then let the tack sit overnight on newspaper so the oil soaks into the leather. Wipe the excess off in the morning with a clean, dry cloth.

Ideally, tack should be wiped off with a moist sponge and saddle soap after each use. The longer the wait between cleanings, the dirtier and more time consuming the job will be. Left dirty too long, the leather may dry out, eventually having to be replaced. (Not a pleasant thought after having spent all that time and money acquiring it.)

Items Needed to Clean Tack

Glycerin or saddle soap	A chamois cloth
Neat's-foot oil or Lexol	Flannel rags
Metal polish	Towel scraps
A stiff brush	An old toothbrush
Tuffy	Wooden matches or tooth
A small natural sponge (not to be used on your horse)	picks

The following is the weekly tack-cleaning routine: Clean the saddle on a sawhorse or other movable rack right in the tack room. Bridles can be draped over a two- or four-pronged hook hanging down from the ceiling. Start with the saddle. If there is any mud on it, let it dry and then brush it off with a stiff brush.

Remove all the saddle's fittings and take the bridle apart. Remember how everything fits together—what attaches to what—so you can put it back together again after it has been cleaned. Soak stirrup irons, curb chain, and bit in warm soapy water while you are cleaning the leather. Then, using a Tuffy and a toothbrush, scrub the dirt buildup from the bit's corners and crevices. Do not use steel wool on the bit because it will leave flakes of iron on the mouthpiece. Wash the stirrups' rubber treads and put them aside to dry.

Soak the girth, if it is washable, and the pads in cool

Your tack should be wiped off after each use.

water and mild soap. Later, machine-wash them in cold water, using a mild soap. Dirty, crusty pads can cause sores, but a strong detergent may irritate the horse's skin. A leather girth should be cleaned with the saddle.

Wash the underside of an English saddle (a Western saddle is lined with real or imitation sheepskin) and leather girth with lukewarm water, mild soap, and rough towel scraps, scrubbing hard to remove all the sweat, dirt, and accumulated hair. It is important not to get leather too wet, so dry it immediately with a chamois cloth.

Then, using the sponge and as little water as possible, apply saddle soap to all leather except an English saddle's suede knee rolls, which can be brushed. Rub the saddle soap in, paying special attention to the heavily stressed areas around the buckles, stirrups, and girth, and let it dry.

Repeat these steps with the bridle and fittings, making sure to wash away the buildup of sweat from the inside of the headstall before applying the saddle soap. Saddle soap is not just a cleaner but a protective, waxlike covering for leather pieces.

While the leather pieces are hanging up to dry, use wooden matches or toothpicks to push the soap and dirt out of the buckle holes.

Polish all metal pieces and shine them with clean pieces of flannel. A light coat of petroleum jelly on the bit will keep it from pitting or rusting when not being used. Using a towel scrap, wipe Lexol or neat's-foot oil into the underside of the saddle's flaps and fenders and into any dry leather except the saddle's seat and outside flaps. This step is not necessary every time the tack is cleaned. Leather will wear and crack without lubrication, but don't overdo it. Too much oil may eventually rot the stitching.

When your youngster has finished scrubbing, brushing, oiling, and shining, help her put everything back together. Tack must be cleaned regularly to keep it soft and pliable.

Weather affects leather, so do not leave tack outside if the temperature drops below freezing. You will also notice that the higher the humidity, the faster leather mildews. Store leather tack on racks in a cool, well-ventilated room away from direct sunlight.

TACK ROOM SETUP

The ideal tack room is one built in the barn, but it can also be in a laundry room, a spare closet, or the corner of a garage. It doesn't have to be elaborate or expensive, just convenient and well organized. Grain cans can also be stored in the tack room.

A secure door with a latch is a necessary precaution if the tack room is located within reach of your horse. A curious horse can cause considerable damage to both himself and your tack by nibbling on leather pieces or prying open the feedbins.

The saddle can be stored on a foldaway steel saddle rack or on a two-by-four wrapped in old pads or feed sacks to protect the leather. Air should be able to circulate underneath the saddle for drying. The saddle pad should hang down in front of the saddle or be laid on top of the saddle upside down so it can dry, too.

The English saddle should be stored with its stirrup irons run up one side of the leathers just below where they are attached to the saddle and with its girth unbuckled and laid flat across the saddle, ends tucked through the irons.

The stirrups on a Western saddle can just hang down in their usual position.

Bridles should not be hung over a single nail, since the sharp bend there can eventually damage the leather. A wooden half-moon, 6 inches across and 1½ inches wide, attached to the wall, curved side up, is perfect for hanging the bridle on.

Heavy pegboard on one wall, with a variety of hooks, will come in handy for those extra bits, straps, and ropes. Brushes, combs, picks, rags, and other grooming equipment can be stored in a pail or a tote box, both of which are easy to carry from place to place or from barn to show.

A roll of paper towels will come in use when you need to wipe your hands, wash the barn windows, or do any of a million odd jobs. Of course, a trashcan is indispensable. Other modern conveniences include a telephone, good lights, radio, and, for those hot summer days, a fan.

For all medicines, ointments, and other first-aid items, an old medicine or kitchen cabinet that can be securely closed should be placed high up on another wall—out of reach of little children.

Blankets, extra tack, bandages, pads, and all the other things that just seem to accumulate can be stored in a secondhand trunk.

A blanket rack across the back of the door or on another wall can be made easily and inexpensively out of a heavy-duty dowel hanging from two ropes, two ½-inch pegs with a nylon rope strung between them, or a piece of hose with a rope strung through it and attached at either end to the wall.

Ingenuity and organization are all that are needed to transform that corner of piled-up tack and equipment into a neatly organized tack room.

The ideal tack room is convenient and well organized.

JODHPURS OR JEANS?

Around the barn and out on the trails, casual jeans and boots or hard shoes are practical and still the most popular riding clothes. Sweatpants with leather knee patches, riding tights, chaps, and leggings are also worn.

Waterproof stable shoes or rubber boots are best for mucking out stalls, sloshing around in spring's inevitable mud, and plowing through winter's snowdrifts. However, rubber is not the best insulation to keep feet warm, so room in the boots for an extra pair of thermal socks during winter months will be necessary.

Safety has always been a concern for parents of horseback riders. Two of the best safety products—one old and one new—are a hard hat and a body protector.

A hard hat with safety harness in place under the chin is a must while jumping, and for safety's sake it should be worn whenever you or your children are riding. A body protector, a kind of vest made to reduce injuries to the body, is growing in popularity, especially with foxhunters and eventers.

WESTERN CLOTHING

Western clothing for a horse show includes boots, a felt (winter) or straw (summer) hat, pants that have a little flare to go over the boots, and a Western shirt. Some participants wear knitted pullover vests or a Western jacket and tie. Chaps should be worn, except in equitation classes.

If your child has good posture, chose one solid color for the shirt, pants, and chaps to highlight it. Questionable posture can be camouflaged by a tailored jacket. Be critical and see what she looks best in—color and style—before you buy. Colors of show clothes often coordinate with the tack and the horse's color, too: A black horse's rider might wear red show clothes, and an Appaloosa's, a bright blue outfit.

ENGLISH CLOTHING

For an English equitation or hunt class your child should wear short jodhpur boots with jodhpurs, or breeches with high boots, and a coat and hard hat. (The rule of thumb is: A child should wear jodhpurs mounted on a pony, breeches when she is riding a horse.) A rat-catcher shirt with choker and stock pin, a white shirt and necktie, or a turtleneck are all acceptable. Gloves are optional, but desirable. Have rubber soles put on boots because they wear better than leather and will improve stirrup grip.

Visit a local horse show with your youngster and see what most of the riders, particularly the winners, are wearing. Certain items are more popular in different areas of the country and styles do change. You have more freedom of choice with Western clothing than you do with English riding clothes. Plain is always better with English tack and togs, while Western riders usually have more color in their riding outfits.

Tightly rolled newspapers or magazines put in your boots when they are not being used will help to keep their shape without the expense of boot trees. Clean your boots, apply boot cream, and periodically use neat's-foot oil on them to prolong their life.

A velvet hard hat should be stored right side up so the velvet doesn't crush and flatten. If it gets rained on, put the hat over a jar or large bottle so nothing mashes down the velvet nap while it dries.

Room and Board for Horses

Horses should be fed according to individual needs. These needs will depend on many things: age and size, health and temperament, the kind and degree of activity, the climate, and the season of the year.

A horse should be fed with a goal of longtime service rather than temporary economy. Ask your vet to help set up your new horse's feeding schedule. If the horse is in good condition, you might ask the former owner what and how much he has been feeding him. Never depend on the instructions on a bag of feed—they have been written to sell more of the company's products.

WHEN TO FEED YOUR HORSE

As important as *what* to feed a horse is *when* to feed him. A horse is a large animal, needing a great deal of food, but with a stomach too small to handle the entire daily nourishment at one time. Food passes rapidly through this small stomach in order to get to the intestines where it is digested, thus making the horse feel almost constantly hungry.

A horse is a grazing animal that prefers to eat small amounts of feed several times a day. He should be fed at least twice and preferably three or four times a day. Divide the daily ration by the number of times you plan to feed. You might give half the grain and hay in the early morning, the other half of the grain in late afternoon, and the rest of the hay before going to bed so your horse has something to nibble on during the night.

This last portion of hay is a good pacifier because horses are kept busy throughout the night. Pastured animals graze; stalled horses are up and down, drinking water, dozing, searching for stray wisps of hay, and wandering about their stalls. The hay also provides an important winter benefit: Besides helping to prevent the early morning empty feeling, giving a portion of hay late in the evening aids in maintaining proper body heat. Digestion causes body heat, which will peak during those chilly predawn hours.

Once the feeding schedule has been set, make sure your family sticks to it. A horse is a creature of habit, so avoid changing the routine. He will be unhappy if his regularly scheduled mealtime is delayed. Feed in this order: water, hay, and then grain. A horse with water in his stall will drink the proper amount without supervision from you.

Seasonal adjustments should be gradual—less grain if

there is an opportunity to get nourishment from fresh grass in the spring and early summer. But a horse that will suddenly be standing idle for even a couple of days after a routine of hard work should have a grain feeding cut down immediately—maybe even in half. Grains are high-energy foods and if you continue to feed the usual amount without the usual work, your horse may get sick and may even suffer azoturia. (See chapter 9.) At the very least, your family pet will have an overabundance of energy, possibly too much for your children to control.

Otherwise, any subtractions from or additions to your horse's diet should be gradual. Be careful when changing from one grain to another. Some grains weigh more and others take up more space. It may require some figuring to come up with the same portions. Institutional-size fruit and vegetable cans and 2-pound coffee cans are convenient measuring containers.

If your horse doesn't have access to water, give him water before giving him grain because the water may wash the food right through his system too fast for the body to retain any of the nutrition. Grain has a tendency to swell when wet, so a horse watered after a grain feeding may even develop a bad case of colic (see chapter 9).

Once you have established what and how much you will feed, keep an eye on your pet's condition to see if he is gaining or losing weight. More backyard horses are too fat rather than too thin because they aren't exercised regularly. Too much of anything—whether it is the right or the wrong food—may cause stomach problems such as colic.

A horse that is fed too much hay will develop a "hay belly," which many veterinarians believe will affect the animal's stamina and respiratory function. However, those that are not fed enough will become thin, with hollow flanks, requiring many months of good feeding to cover their ribs again.

If your horse has a tendency to have leg or foot problems, don't put any extra weight on him. Overweight horses also tend to colic easier.

Before putting your overweight horse on a diet, check with your vet for an opinion. Your horse may look fat to you, but it might just be his type of build. A chunky Quarter Horse may appear overweight next to a lanky thoroughbred or vice versa, but actually they may both be just right.

Some guidelines to remember when feeding a horse:

1. Give several small feedings rather than one large feeding.
2. Feed according to how hard the animal is being worked.
3. Avoid sudden changes in the feeding schedule, and in the kind and amount of food offered.
4. Water the horse first before feeding him.
5. Never feed or water the horse until he is sufficiently cooled off after a workout.
6. Never ride the horse immediately after feeding him.

WHAT TO FEED

Feed is the horse owner's greatest single expense, but costs can be kept down through careful, conscientious feeding rather than through nutrition-depriving shortcuts. Your horse will get out of his food only what is in it, so spend a little more for quality. It will be well worth it. A healthy horse, free of internal parasites, is less expensive to feed than a sickly animal that you are constantly nursing back to health.

Complicated mixtures of expensive rations are not necessary. Most horses will do very well on water, hay, oats, some corn supplemented with salt, and a simple combination of minerals.

Water

Water is essential to good nutrition. It is critical to the circulatory fluids, waste elimination, and digestive and cooling processes of the horse. It should be fresh, clean, and available to your horse at all times unless he is overheated. A mature horse will normally drink 8 to 12 gallons of water a day, and more on a hot day or after a good workout. Don't rush an animal when he is drinking.

A moving stream or stream-fed pond is best for the pasture, but a watering trough is all right, too, if it is periodically scrubbed clean of all encrusted dirt. Certain algae are toxic to horses, and mosquitoes like to breed in water tanks, so frequent dumping and cleaning is important. A small strainer hung nearby is ideal for skimming leaves and grass off the top of the water.

Water buckets can be set inside an old tire to keep them from being tipped over. They should be dumped and refilled with fresh water each day, and checked to make sure there is sufficient water in them during the day.

Snow is too cold to substitute for water in the winter, so break the ice in your horse's water bucket or trough so he can drink whenever he wants to.

Hay

Hay is the single food most consumed by backyard horses. Legume hays, such as alfalfa and clover, are higher in protein, carotene, and minerals than such grass hays as timothy or bluegrass. They are also more expensive and, if given alone, are too rich for most horses. They are usually mixed with a grass hay (clover with timothy is a popular mix), but a good quality timothy hay is usually all that is needed for a backyard horse.

Good hay is never cheap, but buy the best you can afford and you may be able to save on grain. Once you have found a good source of quality hay at a reasonable price (prices vary, according to the area and how good the growing season was), don't lose it. Good hay sources are tougher to find than the proverbial needle in the haystack.

Whether the hay is a legume or a grass, it should be a faded green in color and free of any mold or excessive dustiness. Early-cut hays with a high proportion of leaves to stems are generally higher in nutrition than stemmy, coarse hay cut in the mature stage.

Hay should be properly cured and dried because moldy hay is poisonous and can kill your horse. Rain on cut hay lying in the fields can cause it to spoil and will certainly lessen the quality of it. If baled while wet or soaked while in the bale, hay is absolutely certain to mold and may even cause spontaneous combustion in the hayloft.

Open one or two bales to examine the hay before paying for an order. If the farmer won't allow this, buy a bale or two, open them to see if the hay is fresh and green, not dry, crumbled, or dusty. If you are satisfied, then give your order.

Many barns have been lost due to spontaneous combustion. The only protection is to not stack wet hay but to pile bales on end in open pyramids to allow them to dry. Spoilage may still occur, but the bales are less likely to accumulate sufficient heat to burst into flame.

Bales of hay vary in weight, but all are tied with either

string or wire. Once opened, the bale will fall into sections or "flakes." You can always keep track of how much you feed your horse by how many sections you give him daily. However, do notice that sections may vary in size in the different bales.

Grass

Grass is the natural food of horses. However, hard-working animals need supplemental energy foods, such as oats or a grain mixture (sweet feed sold at feed mills) to keep them fit.

The nutritional value of a pasture depends upon the amount, the maturity, and the type of forage available. As the green grass of spring matures, it increases in fiber and decreases in nutritional value. The dry brown grass of fall and winter is usually low in protein and vitamins, so you will have to give your horse other feeds during those seasons.

A good pasture helps to lower feed costs if enough acreage is available and it is kept free of parasites. A 1- or 2-acre pasture will provide a horse with three to six months' grazing, depending on the weather. (An overly dry spring or summer will cause the grass to turn brown sooner than usual.)

If possible, divide your pasture in half so you can rotate your horse from one side to the other. This will allow each section to rest and recover and help prevent overgrazing. If necessary, you may have to take the horse off the pasture before it is completely grazed bare because overgrazing will damage it for next year's use.

Lawn clippings in the lawn mower bag ferment so quickly that feeding your horse more than a handful or two is mistaken kindness. Beware, too, of hedge clippings and garden wastes because many of them are toxic.

Since toxic sprays are used in many areas, be sure your pasture has not been contaminated by chemicals that have drifted from a nearby orchard or vineyard. For this same reason you should not allow your horse to nibble the grass along a roadside where road maintenance crews might have sprayed. Mow your pasture to keep the weeds under control. Horses will not eat certain weeds unless there is nothing else to eat, and if you do not mow, these weeds will take over where the grass has been eaten down by the horse.

When spring comes and bright green sprouts shoot up all over your horse's field, don't let him out to graze all day right away. Introduce him slowly—an increase of thirty minutes every day up to four hours—until his body can adjust to the extra richness of new grass.

Spring is the season when horses are most susceptible to founder (see chapter 9) because of all the fresh green grass. The causes of grass founder, or laminitis, are unclear, but they are apparently related to the rapid growth of the grasses and to the weather. (Acute cases seem to be more prevalent after a warm spring rain.)

Grass founder can strike horses that live on pasture year-round as well as those that have a sudden change in diet from hay to grass. For some reason, ponies are more apt to founder than are horses. Also, overweight horses founder more quickly than do well-maintained horses. Any horse or pony with a history of founder should be kept off fresh young pastures.

Grains

Grains include oats, corn, barley, wheat, and bran. They are high-energy foods for horses. Ponies don't usually require any grain unless heavily worked and then only a handful or two.

Grain should be clean and bright colored; and oats, plump and full with a sweet smell. A dull gray color indicates musty or moldy oats. Oats are available whole, crimped, or crushed. Whole oats are not so dusty as the other two, and you can see what you are getting, but many horses don't chew them properly. Crimped oats with barley and molasses are good for fussy eaters.

Corn is a good addition to your horse's diet in the winter because it helps to produce body heat. However, do not give any corn if your horse is prone to colic. Corn on the cob is an excellent diversion for nervous or cooped-up horses. Give two large ears of corn at night for your horse to munch on.

Bran, which acts as a laxative, should be given only in small amounts to your horse. A handful mixed in with your horse's daily ration as a dietary supplement is sufficient. If your horse's droppings are too runny, cut back on the bran or meal; and if they're too hard, give more. If the situation doesn't change in a day or two, call your vet.

Hot bran mashes consist of bran, oats, or a mixed feed, salt, molasses, and boiling water for steaming. They are said to be as healing as "mother's chicken soup" and should be served warm. It is not necessary to give them on a regular basis. Most horse owners mix them up and serve them as a treat to their horses after a long day of strenuous activity, such as a fox hunt. Soybean, linseed, and cottonseed meal are protein supplements. They contribute to a glossy coat and are good for the bowels. Add a handful of one to the grain ration three times a week.

Corn oil is an excellent and relatively inexpensive fat source for the horse. It benefits poor hooves and rough, dry coats. Begin giving 1 to 2 ounces per day, and gradually build up to 1 cup per day. However, if you feed him any more, you may interfere with the horse's ability to absorb key vitamins A and E.

Most horses consume their corn oil-coated feed without any problem, but special care will be needed to keep the feed bucket clean: It will quickly build up a coating of oil that can become rancid.

Feeds

Ready-mixed or sweet feeds are usually easier to store (everything is in one can rather than each individual grain in separate cans) and less time-consuming for the single horse owner to prepare than keeping on hand all the different grains. They are more expensive but do provide a well-rounded diet with a combination of grains, salt, fish meal, linseed, assorted trace minerals, and, if a sweet feed, molasses. Either one is a good choice, although in winter the sweet feed may become hard as a rock if the temperature goes low enough.

Pelleted feeds for horses have become very popular in recent years. They are made from several different combinations of grain and hay, and take the place of both. Their advantages include: a more balanced ration; less waste; no dust to irritate horses with respiratory diseases such as the heaves (see chapter 9); less bulk to ship, handle, and store; and no lost leaves, as happens when such hays as clover and alfalfa are mashed together.

The cost of pellets is the biggest disadvantage. However, this factor may be offset by the high price a single horse owner may have to pay for a few bales of hay because he has very little storage space.

Pellets also contribute to wood chewing in horses that

are confined. This nervous habit can be reduced, however, by including some hay—necessary for roughage—with the daily ration of pellets to give the horse something else to chew.

Salt Blocks

Salt blocks, which should also be available for your horse to lick freely year-round, can be bought at your local feed store or tack shop. Salt helps the body retain moisture, prevents dehydration, and aids in the breaking down of nutrients and the filtering of wastes. It is especially important in the summer when the heat makes a horse sweat a great deal.

Place a large block in your pasture under a shelter so the rain won't erode it. A smaller one goes in your horse's stall, either in a plastic holder on the wall or in his feed bucket. On the average, a horse will need about one pound of salt a week. Use iodized salt in geographic areas that are iodine deficient.

PROBLEM EATERS

A horse that bolts his feed should be discouraged from continuing this habit. To do so, place a tennis-ball-size rock in his dish to slow him down. You can also give him his hay first to take the edge off his appetite.

Finding whole grains of corn and oats in your horse's manure is a good indication of bolting. A horse with this habit does not get the full value of his food.

Picky eaters need some chopped-up carrots and a little molasses, sugar, or honey added to their grain to entice them to clean up their feed bins. Other vegetables (such as turnips and sugar beets) and fruits (such as peaches, apples, and pears) will also encourage them to eat. Cut up the fruit, removing all pits. Do not overfeed with these tantalizers—no more than two apples a day.

BEDDING

Horses confined in a stall need good clean bedding daily because, although they do a lot of napping standing up, they also like to lie down to rest.

There are several materials that you can use to bed your horse down. They all have their advantages and disadvantages, which may differ according to what part of the country you live in and what is available.

Straw, wood shavings, and sawdust are the most commonly used materials. Straw provides good drainage, dries fastest, and looks clean and fresh. However, some horses may try to eat it. Being bulky, it also creates bigger manure piles and needs more room for storage. In certain parts of the country, there are mushroom growers who will be glad to come and haul manure and soiled straw away for their mushroom flats.

Wood shavings and sawdust are available at little or no cost in some areas, but you might have to bag and transport them back to your barn yourself. The price on those already bagged for you has gone up considerably in the last couple of years. The easiest to use are kiln-dried, little flakes so they fall easily through your fork when cleaning the stall. There is more waste with the bigger flakes.

Sawdust may be dusty, not very absorbent, and mat down quickly, so you have to use more for a soft bed. Make sure the shavings and sawdust you use are not made from black walnut; it is very toxic to horses and can cause severe laminitis.

Never buy or use moldy hay for bedding, because your horse will eat it and stand a good chance of being poisoned.

STORAGE

To eliminate constant trips to a farmer or dealer for more hay, you will need a large storage area. It will also be cheaper as well as more convenient if you can buy a year's supply at one time, about 1 ton for one horse. Buy your supply in summer or early fall to get the lowest price.

Share the cost and divide an order of hay and/or grain with a friend or two if you have limited space for storage or think the food will be too old by the time your horse gets to the bottom of the barrel. Some feed dealers will deliver your order free of charge if you buy a minimum number of pounds of grain or bales or tons of hay.

A storage area for hay and bedding can be on the second floor of your barn, in a room next to the stall, or even in a separate building. The area should be kept dry so that its contents do not become moldy.

Air should be allowed to circulate under hay bales to lessen the chance of spontaneous combustion. Pile the bales onto a wooden pallet or framework of thick boards a few inches from the floor. A thick layer of old hay from the previous year's bales will also allow some air circulation, so don't sweep your barn clean when you're expecting a new shipment.

Never stack the bales too close to a light bulb. The heat from the bulb may start a fire. A wire shield several inches in diameter around each bulb will keep you from accidentally stacking the hay too close to them.

Grain should be stored in closed containers, such as garbage cans with tight-fitting lids. Galvanized metal is stur-

Grain should be stored in closed containers with tight-fitting tops so that a loose horse can't get into it.

dier than plastic but needs a plastic bag liner because the feed causes the metal to rust.

Be sure that all the grain is used up in the can before you dump a fresh bag in. If it isn't finished, empty the remains out into another container and then put this older portion on top of the new grain so you will use it first. The bottom grain can become moldy and make your horse very sick—even kill him—if you hold it over until the end of another order.

Remember: What you put into your horse is what you will get out of him. Conscientious, consistent care will keep him happy and healthy and a good companion on a fine day of trail riding with other horse-owning friends.

6

Grooming Steed and Stall

Caring for a horse is time consuming and just plain hard work. Keeping a horse in good condition—healthy and well groomed—should be satisfying work for your children, however, especially when they know that their horse is fit enough to enjoy a ride as much as they do.

As a horse owner your child will spend many more hours brushing, picking, washing, clipping, shoveling, sweeping, and feeding than riding. However, this is the time that she will also have a chance to really get to know her horse's habits, quirks, likes, and dislikes.

STABLE EQUIPMENT

In order to care for a horse properly you will have to go shopping with your child to buy the special equipment listed on page 94.

For Grooming

A rubber currycomb

A stiff dandy brush

A soft dandy brush or body
   brush

A large plastic comb for tail

A metal mane comb

Clean towels

A sweat scraper

A shedding blade

A bucket

Horse shampoo

Coat conditioner

3 sponges (2 small, 1 large)

Fly repellent

A hoof pick

Hoof dressing

Body clippers (optional)

A stepping stool

For Stall Cleaning

A manure fork

A pitchfork

A flat-ended shovel

A broom

A dustpan

A rake

A wheelbarrow or garden
   cart

A manure basket

Hydrated lime

Other Equipment

Wire clippers

A hammer

Pliers

A screwdriver

A leather punch

A trashcan

A fire extinguisher

These items can be bought at a tack shop, hardware store, or feed store. The cleaning equipment can be stored in an alcove or corner. Put hooks on the walls so most tools can be hung up.

GETTING TO KNOW YOUR HORSE

The day the new horse arrives and takes his place in your backyard will be one of ecstasy and joy for your youngster, but confusing and possibly frightening to the horse. The animal will need time to get used to the new surroundings. Love and attention will help.

When you approach a strange horse, do so slowly and cautiously, but confidently. Try not to be nervous or afraid, because a horse can sense your feelings and may react accordingly—either just as fearfully or bullying.

Let the horse sniff your hand. Then pet him firmly on the neck or shoulder, never a timid stroke on the nose, which most horses hate.

It will be up to your family to reassure and welcome the horse to his new home. Start by letting him become accustomed to his new family. Always move slowly; never dart or sneak around a horse. Give plenty of warning of your next action: a pat on the rump before walking behind him, a few words as you pass by carrying a saddle, bridle, or other miscellaneous equipment. Startling the animal could prompt a kick.

Your child should spend as much time as she can with the horse, working around him and introducing him to the barn, paddock, or pasture, the tack, and especially to her. She might sit outside the stall and do her homework, read a book nearby while the horse grazes, or just stand at the stall door and talk. Continuous chattering is pleasing to a horse, and even a radio's rock music and DJ's nonsense is soothing.

A new horse will usually be too excited and not comfortable enough yet to lie down at night in an unfamiliar stall, but this is natural. It may take a few days, even a couple of months, before he relaxes enough to take advantage of that fresh, soft bed you slaved over.

If there is another horse already in your backyard, do not turn them out together until they get to know each other. Instead, ride them side by side in the ring or out on the trail. Turn them out in adjoining paddocks so they can meet each other over the fence. When you do eventually put them in the same field, watch for any signs of trouble.

There will probably be some initial squealing and kicking up of heels, but this is to be expected until the pecking order is established. The pecking order is a social system that establishes which animal is the leader, which is second in line, and so on down to the last horse, who knuckles under to all the others. The most aggressive and cleverest horse, rather than the biggest and strongest, usually ends up as the Big Cheese.

If possible, have the two horses' hind shoes removed before turning them out together. Usually this isn't practical to do, but horses without shoes will do less damage to each other if a kick does connect during this testing period.

GROOMING

Grooming is an important part of horse keeping that should be done before and after every ride. It stimulates circulation, contributes to good muscle tone, and puts the sheen in a horse's coat.

Even a horse that is not ridden should be groomed every couple of days. Accumulated dirt on a horse left out for the winter acts as an insulator against cold winds and freezing temperatures, but an occasional brushing will keep his coat in better condition. Grooming also gives the owner a chance to check for cuts and other injuries.

The most convenient way to groom a horse is to put him in crossties. The ideal place is in a hallway or covered area outside the stall, but if you do not have such a spot, then

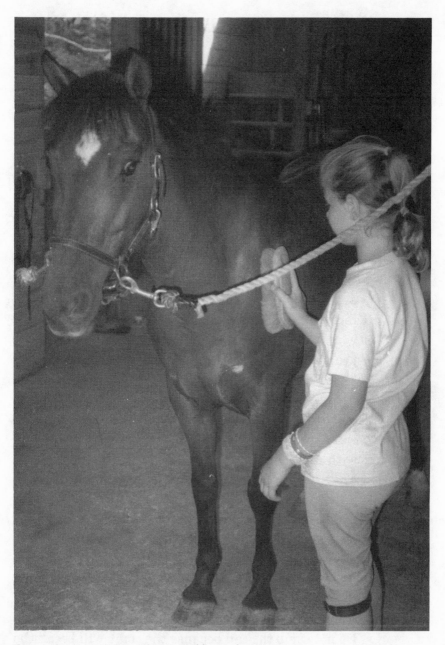

Grooming is an important part of horse keeping.

crosstie him in his stall, or, in nice weather, between two trees.

Grooming should be done in old clothes because the dust will fly if grooming is done properly. Your child may end up with a fine film of dust all over herself.

There are numerous ways in various sequences to groom a horse, but the logical place to start is at the top. Work down and from front to back, starting at the top of the neck just behind the ears and working back to the tail. Never stand directly behind the horse. Clean the tail by pulling it around and stand to the side at the horse's hip.

1. Using the rubber currycomb at the top of the neck on the "near" (or left) side, rub it in a circular motion against the hair. Do so all over the horse's body to remove dried mud and caked-on sweat. Be careful of your horse's sensitive flanks and girth area. Do not use the currycomb on your horse's face or below his knees and hocks.

    Knock the dirt and old hair out of the currycomb by banging it face down on a hard surface, such as a wall, post, or door. (You can later brush the marks off with a broom.)

2. The stiff dandy brush should be used next to brush away the dirt loosened by the currycomb and to clean the legs from the knees and hocks down. Brush with the hair in short strokes. Do not use this brush on the horse's face.

    Clean the brush frequently by rubbing it against the currycomb.

3. Using the metal comb, comb the mane and forelock. Do not comb the tail because the comb will break the long hairs, and the tail will soon be thin and wispy.

Cleaning your horse's feet is part of daily grooming.

Use your fingers to carefully remove shavings or burrs from the tail.

4. Use the soft dandy brush or the body brush on the horse's face and ears, shielding his eyes one at a time with your free hand to prevent dust from blowing into them.

Then go over the rest of his body, cleaning the soft brush against the stiff one as you work.

5. Wipe the horse with a clean towel to give the coat an extra glow.

6. Starting with the left front foot, clean the horse's feet with a hoof pick. (Tap or press on the lower leg, telling the horse to "lift" or "pick up," to encourage him to pick up his foot.) Facing the horse's tail, hold the hoof with your left hand and support it on your left

knee. Pick away from you along each side of the frog (triangular horny pad on the sole of the foot) to remove any packed mud, manure, or bedding.

Clean the left hind foot next, then the right front and right rear ones.

7. Take a small damp sponge and wipe away any secretions from eyes and nostrils.

8. During the fly season, spray or wipe on fly repellent. Never spray around the horse's face.

A thorough grooming as described above should always be given the horse before anyone rides him. If the horse is cooled off after being ridden, he needs only a light brushing. A damp body sponge is good for removing the sweat and salt that have accumulated under and around the saddle, girth, and bridle (sponging also seems to speed up the drying process).

Lead the horse around to dry after sponging. Do not turn him out, for he will immediately roll in the dirt. On a cool day, rub him with towels and then walk him. If he is still damp, put a cooler or blanket on him and push handfuls of straw up under the blanket to keep it away from his back so air can circulate.

Finally, wash your brushes, combs, and other grooming equipment once a week so they don't make your clean horse dirty.

BATHING

Your youngster will probably want to bathe her horse sometime, either before a show, after a hard ride on a hot day, or just on some warm afternoon when she feels like giving her pet the works.

She shouldn't bathe him more than once a week. It is not necessary to bathe a horse often, because daily grooming will keep his coat quite healthy. Instead of frequent all over baths, spot-wash any white areas that are stained, or use a Vetrolin body brace followed by a lukewarm rinse. Bathing a horse removes dandruff, dirt, and manure stains, but it also removes the natural oil from the coat, so it will not be as glossy for a day or two.

Do not wash a horse in cold weather, and if your youngster bathes your horse the day before a show, use a coat of conditioner afterward to bring out the sheen again.

1. If there is a hose available, attach to it a rubber or plastic currycomb made for this purpose, then rub in a circular motion, with the water running, to draw out the dirt next to the horse's skin.

2. Mix up a pail of warm water and antibacterial soap and, with the body sponge, wash around the horse's face and ears. Wring out the sponge so the soapy water doesn't drip into his eyes or ears. Rinse carefully; most horses hate to have water sprayed in their face and around their heads.

3. Starting at the top of the horse's neck, scrub with the sponge to remove any stains. Wash a section (neck and chest) at a time, working the soap up into a good lather. Rinse as you go, so the soap isn't left too long to dry out the horse's skin.

4. Wash the mane, brushing it over to the right or off side with the stiff dandy brush if you ride your horse English style. (It may be on either side if you ride Western.) Then do the tail, dipping the entire tail into the bucket so you can really scrub down to the bone to clean it.

Rinse well, looking for ticks. Remove any that you find, and thoroughly clean the area with soap and water. Then apply a small amount of iodine, and watch over the next several days to make sure no infection sets in. In addition to causing skin problems, ticks transmit diseases, including Lyme disease.

If your horse's tail has flakes of dry skin, massage a dandruff shampoo into it, leaving it on the skin for ten minutes before rinsing. (See chapter 9, which discusses tail rubbing.)

5. Next spray the tail with a tangle-free solution. When the tail has dried, use the plastic comb to carefully comb the tail out. Do a section at a time, trying not to break any hairs. Do not brush or comb the tail every day but do so only for special occasions.

6. Last, wash the horse's lower legs and the hoofs. Rinse your horse off well, either with a hose or several pails of water. Add a cup of vinegar to the rinse water in a bucket to cut the soapsuds.

7. Use a sweat scraper to scrape off any excess water on his body. Do not use this metal device on the face or legs.

8. Dry the face with a clean towel and wipe the underside of the horse's belly from both sides. Run the towel down the legs, squeezing out excess water. Make sure to dry the area below the fetlock extra carefully so the skin doesn't chap and cause scratches (see chapter 9).

9. Immediately put a cooler on the horse and walk him until he is dry all over. Don't leave him tied or loose where he can lie down or roll.

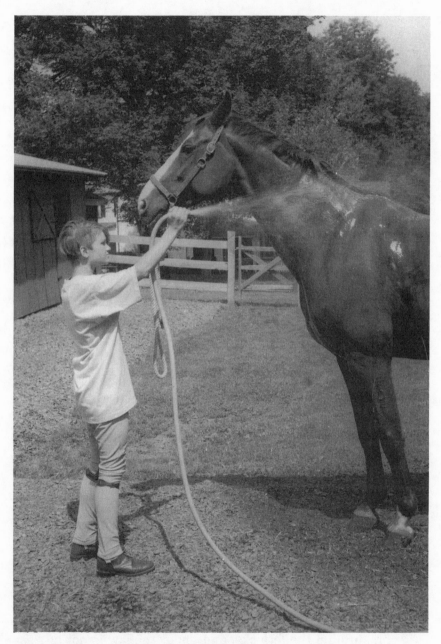

Rinse your horse off well after bathing him.

Hoof dressing may be applied to the hooves once or twice a week to keep them pliable and to improve their appearance before a show. Do not put it on more often because too much will have the opposite effect and seal moisture out.

On an English horse, a mane that won't stay down on the right side should be brushed over to the correct side every time you groom him. One that refuses to stay in place or one with sections that don't stay in place can be dampened with a sponge, braided in little braids and left pulled over to the correct side with the weight of the braids to hold the hair down for a day or two. But watch your horse to see that the braids don't irritate him. If they do, he will rub his neck to get them out and rub off chunks of the mane, too.

Never cut your horse's mane with a scissors except over the poll where the bridle goes. To shorten a mane, it has to be "pulled" by backcombing a small section and then pulling out the three to six longest hairs remaining in your fingers. It doesn't hurt the horse if you don't pull too many at one time. If your horse fusses, don't do his mane all at one time. Instead, try shortening a section at a time over a couple of days.

Some Western horses have their manes roached (cut off) except for the forelock and a handhold at the withers. This must be done with clippers, up one side of the neck, up the other and then up the middle.

Before using electric clippers on your horse, turn them on and hold them next to him for a few minutes every day to get your pet used to their sound and looks. Make sure they are sharp and clean so they don't catch and pull the hair.

Trimming is a job for an expert, and clipping out the ears, around the fetlocks, and under the jaw is not an easy

Trim your horse's whiskers with electric clippers.

job. Have someone experienced with clipping show you how so you don't make the animal clipper-shy.

Approximately four times a year clean a mare's udder and the entrance to a gelding's sheath with warm soapy water and a small sponge. Rub gently to remove the accumulation of dirt and a black substance called smegma. Rinse well.

Stand to the side and as far forward as you can so you are not kicked. Watch your horse's ears to see if the washing irritates him. If you are uncertain how to clean the sheath, ask your vet or a knowledgeable friend to show you.

A horse that is kept blanketed during the winter will not grow so heavy a coat as one left uncovered. Even so, by spring a one- or two-handled shedding blade will come in handy to scrape off the mounds of loose hair. Use it lightly on the flanks and stomach and not at all on the face or lower legs.

Keep your grooming equipment all together in a tote box, bucket, old trunk, or box on a shelf, or in the compartments of an old shoebag. A grooming box on the wall next to the crossties is very handy. Don't leave brushes or other equipment underfoot while you groom because you or your horse may step on them. Put them away after you use them and they will never be "missing."

HOOVES

A horse's feet and their care are a very important part of horse hygiene. Feet should be kept clean and not allowed to dry out. They should be trimmed and shod when shoes are necessary for riding on hard surfaces. A horse who cannot put any weight on an injured or sore foot will not be able to

Your horse's hooves should be trimmed every four to six weeks by a competent farrier.

walk, because he cannot limp on three legs as a dog or cat can; thus the saying "No foot, no horse."

Clean a stabled or worked horse's feet daily, checking for loose shoes, stones in the feet, or thrush (see chapter 9).

Loose shoes are seen more often in the spring, and if there is deep mud in the pasture, they'll pull right off. If a shoe is lost, you will have to buy a new shoe, so to eliminate this expense, inspect the shoes every day. Keep your horse in his stall until the farrier comes if a shoe is loose or comes off; exercise or even just running around without a shoe will break off the edges of the foot.

Hooves should be trimmed every four to six weeks, whether your horse is shod or not. They grow just as your fingernails do, and untrimmed feet may cause toeing in or out, thus altering the way your horse moves by putting unnatural stress on his legs.

Shoes can be reset several times before new shoes are needed. A competent blacksmith makes new shoes to fit the foot, not the foot to fit the shoe.

Shoes are also used to change gaits, correct faulty hoof structure or growth, and aid a hoof that has corns, contracted heels, or cracks. Leather or synthetic pads and shoes with borium cushion the feet and give horses better traction on roads and in ice and snow.

CLEANING STALLS

Cleaning stalls strengthens your muscles, builds character, and clears out your sinuses. Stalls that are cleaned daily are more healthful for your horse and easier and more economical for you to maintain. In fact, picking up the piles of manure periodically during the day if the horse is indoors will make the job simpler and less time consuming.

Establish a stall-cleaning routine. Horses prefer a set routine and, by doing things in the same order every day, you will save time. Organization and planning are essential to a good routine. Having the right amount of supplies is also part of the routine. Always put things away in the same place so you never waste time hunting for them.

The easiest way to clean your horse's stall is to do it when he is outside. However, if the weather isn't cooperating, you can tie him to one side in the stall, put him on the crossties or just give him some hay in the corner so he will stand to one side.

Remove the obvious piles of manure first and then sift through the bedding with the manure fork to pick up loose balls of manure that may have been scattered about by the horse's feet. If you are faithful about picking up the manure at least once a day you will probably only have to "strip" or clean the stall really well once a week. This job requires a little more time and muscle.

1. Pick up all the manure with the manure fork and put it in the wheelbarrow or manure basket.

2. Using the manure fork, carefully scrape all the dry bedding to the sides but leave the wet areas exposed. (If your horse is a gelding, the wet area will be in the center of the stall; if a mare, the wet area will probably be to the back or one side of the stall). Save as much dry bedding as you can.

3. Using a pitchfork, dig all the wet bedding out of the stall and load it into the wheelbarrow. Depending on your schedule, you may leave the wet floor uncovered for the rest of the day to dry out. Open doors and windows to air the barn out even on cold days.

4. Sprinkle lime on a clay or dirt floor or wash an asphalt or cement one with disinfectant to kill the germs that give the stall a foul odor. Don't let your horse get to either the lime or the disinfectant. Rinse the floor well of all the disinfectant, then pull all the old bedding back over the area where the lime was sprinkled before putting your horse back in the stall.

   Add a bale or large bag of new bedding so it is deep enough for a horse to lie down in comfortably. Use more in winter for warmth.

5. Sweep the aisle and tack room for a neater appearance. Scrub water and grain buckets.

6. Occasionally knock all the cobwebs down with a broom, dust mop or shop vac. Some people feel that webs help to keep flies under control, but repellent,

sticky paper, and screens or closed doors and windows when the sunlight streams in do a neater and better job. Windows should be washed periodically so there is more natural light in the barn and so the horse can see out.

Turn your horse out as much as possible, and you won't use as much bedding. Your horse will be happier, if the weather is nice, and you will be happier because you will have less cleaning to do. Your horse need only come into the barn on cold winter days and nights or on hot summer days. Make sure he has shade during the warmer days and plenty of fresh water every day.

LONGEING

Longeing, or exercising a horse on a long line, is an excellent way to give your horse some exercise if you are short of time and unable to ride. It's also a great warmup before riding to get the kinks and bucks out of your mount. Twenty minutes is usually sufficient time for a warmup. Attach a long line to the halter's ring under the chin. Walk your horse in a small circle, gradually giving him more line so that you are making an even smaller circle as he walks around you on the outside.

Keep moving backward to the center of your circle, giving him more line until you are turning in place. A long whip, usually just shown to him or waved at him (not for hitting) will keep him away from you and continuing to move. As he gets the idea, you can let out more line until the circle is larger.

If he starts to come in to you, wave the whip in his face.

You may have to start over a few times before he gets the idea.

Never allow the horse to walk into the center when you wish to stop or change directions. Instead, you go out to him. If, after several attempts, the horse still doesn't understand what you want him to do, have your child or a friend lead him around you in a circle until he does. If this method fails, and he still will not do what you want, stop before you lose patience, and try again the next day.

After the horse has been walking around you in a circle on his own for a while, you may start him trotting. Crack or wave the whip and tell him, "Trot." Say the commands "walk," "trot," or "whoa" very clearly and with authority. With practice the horse will change gaits on voice commands alone.

When he has learned to walk, trot, and halt in both directions, you may start him cantering. This is a little more difficult, because you will also have to get him on the correct lead.

Give him the command, "Canter," and crack the whip so he will take the inside or correct lead. Most horses have a favorite lead so start with that one first and praise him when he does it correctly. Then turn the horse in the opposite direction and try the same method to get the other lead, praising him if he does it correctly. But, if he absolutely refuses to take the other lead after several attempts, finish the lesson with something he does do well and try again the next day. You may eventually have to have your riding teacher or a knowledgeable friend help you to get your horse to use both leads if you cannot do it alone.

Do not make your horse go around and around in the same direction, or he will become bored and you dizzy. Keep the circles a good size (about 15–20 meters) and change directions frequently so the pressure isn't always on the muscles of the same or inside leg. Twenty minutes is long enough for longeing.

Never wrap the longe line around your hand or waist to take up the slack. If something should startle the horse, he could turn and run, dragging you if you can't get loose. Wear gloves to prevent blisters if your horse pulls or jerks on the line.

Horse
Etiquette

A HORSE'S MAKEUP

The horse has been a faithful companion to man for centuries. The animal's strength, speed, and stamina have been valuable and useful ever since he became domesticated. The horse has taken his place alongside man throughout history—helping to fight wars, winning games in various sports, working to tame frontiers, pulling the plow to till land, and carrying his master, often for only an hour or two, away from civilization's tensions and headaches into nature's peace and beauty.

A horse is naturally skittish and timid. Flight, rather than fight, was the horse's defense against its predators during the years of evolution, and this is still a very strong instinct. Every impulse tells a horse to turn and run at the slightest danger, or what may seem dangerous. Sometimes this "danger" is no more than a rock, a puddle's reflection, a rabbit hopping across the path, or a sheet flapping on a clothesline.

A horse that shies should be reassured, not punished. Encourage him with strong leg pressure and a light hand to go forward past the frightening object, talking as you go. Angry words and blows will only frighten the animal more. But don't go overboard in petting and praising or the horse may decide that since you're making such a fuss there must really be a danger.

Another tendency dating back from the horse's past is the desire to remain with the herd. A horse dislikes being alone, and if there are no other horses around, he will be happier with a stablemate, such as a cat, rabbit, donkey, goat, or even a chicken.

Some horses are so herd-bound that it is almost impossible to ride them away from the barn or out on a trail without the company of other horses. They know that there is safety in numbers and will refuse to leave their fellow equines. A confirmed herd-bound animal is not for a novice rider, but one with only a slight tendency may be changed by building up his confidence and working on going out alone to encourage boldness.

Horses are not big dogs, with the intellect and devotion of a canine. They are horses, in spite of what some people will try to tell you. However, they are far smarter than most other animals, and with repetition and competent training they can be taught to do many things: cut a steer out of the rest of a herd; perform artificial gaits like the rack; perform difficult dressage movements such as the *passage* and *piaffe;* hold a lasso taut after a calf has been roped;

learn circus tricks; or carry a rider over a 6-foot jump.

Horses cannot reason. If they see a strange object along-side the ring with their right eye as they are going around to the left and shy at it, they will shy again when going around to the right. They can't reason that if the object didn't hurt them when the right eye saw it, it won't hurt them when the left eye sees it. This lack of reasoning makes many people who don't know anything about horses (and some that do) say that horses are dumb. Far from it, however.

Except for the elephant, horses remember more and better than any other animal. They also learn very fast—even faster than dogs—and once taught, they will remember forever. Unfortunately, this applies to bad manners as well as good manners.

Horses are not devoted to people as dogs are. Some

Horses are happier with company and get along well with stablemates of other species such as goats.

whinny when their owners approach, nuzzle them with obvious affection, or come when they are called, but most transfer such actions to whoever next feeds and cares for them. A few really do seem to care for their owners, but the horse's familiarity with and confidence in that person are a probable explanation.

As with most species, horses have individual personalities. Some that are definitely "people horses" are more responsive to people. Others exhibit a strong desire to lead, whether they are in a horse race or on a trail ride. Still others—not necessarily the biggest and strongest—are aggressive and dominate their companions when turned out in a field together.

Some horses love to jump while others become wild-eyed when faced with anything over 18 inches high. Some enjoy strutting in front of a horse show audience, and others are content to plod happily along behind their comrades. A horse's makeup depends on his age, sex, and breeding, but can be affected by his training and experiences.

PRAISE AND PUNISHMENT

A well-mannered horse is a pleasure to own. A spoiled, nasty animal is untrustworthy, no fun, and potentially dangerous to your family.

Make sure your family treats your horse with consideration and kindness. If a winter-cold bit is shoved into your horse's mouth or his tongue is burned on a bit left out in the hot sun, he will begin to fight every time his bridle is put on. If his girth is jerked tight when being saddled, your horse will quickly learn to relieve the pinching and "punch" by blowing up or expanding his barrel, an annoying habit that is impossible to break once learned.

When correction is necessary, discipline the horse firmly, but not cruelly, with a stern "No," a sharp whack, or both. Never hit your horse in the face or he will soon become head-shy and jerk his head up whenever you move your hand. A head-shy horse is a nuisance to bridle, halter, clip, and even groom. Prolonged beating or whipping will only frighten him and may even ingrain the action into a repertoire of tricks.

A horse should be corrected immediately after he disobeys. Even a moment later will be too late. A horse will connect punishment with the bad behavior only if it is administered during or immediately after the action. If your horse runs into you while being led, for instance, give a good jerk on the lead rope and/or a smack on the chest or shoulder immediately to teach him to respect your space. The same punishment a moment or two later will have no meaning to the horse.

Never pit your muscles against those of your horse. Superior strength will win the tug-of-war every time. Instead, use your head to make your horse do what you want—brains over brawn.

CONTRIBUTING TO VICES

As mentioned before, most vices that horses have are caused by people.

A horse that nips may have been fed by hand—carrots, apples, sugar—whenever his owner approached him. A tidbit as a reward is acceptable, but give it to your horse in his feed bucket. A horse that expects constant handouts will become annoyed when they're not given and will nip to remind you.

Never teach your horse to find the goody in your pocket or to accept it from between your teeth. A nip on the hip by a frustrated horse who is attempting to retrieve a carrot from your pocket is painful, but hardly as disfiguring as the loss of the tip of your nose (which actually happened to a young lady who taught her horse to take a piece of carrot from her mouth!).

Be especially careful of what tricks you intentionally teach your horse. Teaching him to stand quietly when being tacked up or mounted, to lift his feet one at a time to be cleaned, or to come when he is called is practical and helpful, but some circus-type stunts may cause unnecessary accidents.

A neighbor thought it would be fun to teach his horse to wave a small white towel on command (since the horse liked to toss one around whenever one was within reach anyway). He changed his mind when his horse grabbed a towel and flung his head up, socking the neighbor in the jaw and almost knocking him out.

Do not teach your horse to rear on a given signal. Rearing is very dangerous to horse and rider. If a horse wearing a saddle falls over backward during a rear, he will probably break the saddle's tree. It's not uncommon for a horse to break his neck, too. You may think you look like the Lone Ranger on Silver, but if your pet ever rears unexpectedly or loses his balance and goes over backward, you may end up looking like a mummy encased in a wad of bandages.

Pawing the ground to tell his age may start your horse pawing in his stall out of boredom or pawing anywhere he is standing because he is impatient. Pawing is an annoying habit and one that could eventually loosen a shoe, resulting in an extra visit and fee from your blacksmith.

Let the instructors at the Spanish Riding School in

Vienna teach *caprioles, levades,* and *courbettes* to their beautiful white Lipizzans. You stick to everyday stable etiquette.

VICES AND HOW TO COPE WITH THEM

Often a horse disobeys because of not knowing what is expected. Even a well-trained horse can be confused if the correct signal is not given.

If you discover why a horse has a particular habit or performs a certain action, you are halfway to the solution. Many horses pick up vices, such as cribbing (wood-chewing), weaving, windsucking, or kicking the walls because they are bored from standing all day in their stalls.

The simplest solutions include turning them out more often, giving them additional exercise, hanging a ball or plastic milk jug in their stall for them to bat around, or doling out their daily hay in several small portions rather than in one or two big feedings to keep them occupied longer. A collar may have to be used on a confirmed windsucker, and metal covers or nasty-tasting (but nontoxic) paints put on all exposed wood to discourage a wood chewer.

If your horse blows up when his girth is tightened, take the girth up a little at a time. You will never break this bad habit, but this way will be easier for you. Take the girth up a hole or two, do something else, and then come back and take it up another hole. Walk your horse out to where you mount and take the girth up a hole again. Mount and you can probably take it up still another hole. After you've ridden for a few minutes, check the girth again and tighten it further if necessary. You want your girth tight enough to keep the saddle from slipping, but not so tight that it is squeezing the horse in two.

Sound like a lot of extra work? Not really. This method takes very little energy compared to trying to get the girth up five or six holes all at once by pitting your strength against your horse's. This way you use your brains instead of your brawn.

If your horse refuses to stand while you are mounting, have someone hold the bridle at first. Work up to mounting by yourself with the horse headed into the corner of a wall or fence so he can't go anywhere. Tell him to stand each time while you practice getting off and on, always praising the horse when he stands quietly.

Soon you will be able to mount anywhere, but never let the horse walk off before you tell him to, or else he will quickly revert to his old habit. Make sure when you mount that you are not poking your horse in the belly with your toe or landing on his back like a 200-pound sack of potatoes, both of which will certainly cause fidgeting, if not down-right mutiny.

After mounting, adjust your stirrups, reins, and girth while making your horse stand still so he learns not to move off as soon as you have swung your leg over his back. Other riders in your group should wait until you have mounted and are ready before starting to walk away. No horse will stand still if his companions are leaving him.

Don't be embarrassed to use a mounting block. It's easier for you and better for your horse's back, and it lessens the chance of a loose saddle being pulled to one side. A stump or large rock are often the perfect height. You can also make a simple wooden mounting block with steps (and even paint it to match your barn colors).

If your horse bites at you, punish him immediately with a slap or whack of a crop on the shoulder, chest or neck. As said earlier, never hit your horse on the head, as this will cause head-shying, another bad habit. The slap should be hard enough to hurt. Scold him loudly at the same time. If you don't let him know that you dislike such actions, the animal may really hurt you or your children someday. The key to this discipline is to do it *immediately,* not five seconds later.

A horse that rears should be quickly discouraged from doing so. Some trainers spin the horse in a circle when they feel him start to rear, but most try to push the horse forward so he doesn't rear. Hitting the horse on the head, once thought to cure this bad habit, usually only makes the horse wilder and more uncontrollable. Calming and talking now prove to have better results. A martingale or tie-down helps to control rearing, but if your horse does rear, lean as far forward as you can and let the reins go slack so you don't pull him over backward. Squeeze with your legs to urge him forward when he comes down so he doesn't go up again. Check for a too small bit or bridle, or teeth that should be filed, before you condemn your horse altogether.

A horse that refuses to be led is rare, but there are some that walk into you, pull back on the lead, or toss their heads, yanking the rope out of your hands. Practice leading your horse so he learns to do it correctly and mannerly.

Always lead from the left (or "near") side, with your right hand on the lead rope about 8 to 10 inches from the halter and your left hand holding the slack. Give a jerk on the lead and scold the horse whenever he walks into you. Praise him when he leads nicely.

Turn your horse by pushing the animal around away from you. Never pull the horse toward you unless you want to risk having your toes stepped on. To help avoid this pain and injury, always wear hard shoes, not sandals or sneakers, in the barn and when you're working around horses.

Walk briskly beside your horse. Never walk backward in front of the animal; many horses will stop and refuse to move if you are facing them. Do not wrap the lead rope around your wrist or hand. If something should startle him and he bolts, you could get a terrific rope burn or even be dragged along behind him.

A horse that eats bedding, the walls of the stall, or even his own manure may have a mineral deficiency, worms, or not enough bulk food (hay). These habits may also be caused by boredom or just plain hunger pangs if the horse is not fed enough. Call your vet for an opinion if your horse does any of these things.

If your horse kicks occasionally, tie the animal in crossties when you are grooming him, and do not walk too closely behind him. Be sure to stand to the side of his hindquarters where he can't reach you with a "cow kick." Swishing the tail and laying the ears back are signals that a kick may be coming.

Nothing is more annoying than to be walking along and suddenly be pulled forward or to one side while your horse grabs at a mouthful of grass or leaves. It's also embarrassing to be pulled out of the saddle, down the horse's neck, and onto the ground in a heap when he suddenly decides to graze. If you have a horse that puts his head down to graze every chance he gets, or snatches leaves from trees along the trail, you should be ready to correct him every time. Once learned, this is a hard habit to break. Keep a firm grip on the reins, but not too heavy a pressure on his mouth. If the horse does succeed in snatching a mouthful, say "no" immediately and smack his shoulder with the crop or whip. Expect a startled jump.

Don't allow your horse to use you as a scratching post for his hot, itchy head after riding. A firm "no" and a slap on the neck can save you quite a cleaning bill and possibly even a hard knock on the head. After you have taken the bridle off, be sure to rub around his ears and mouth with an old towel to relieve his itching.

Hard to catch in the field? Set up your routine so you ride before you put your horse out or after you bring him in for feeding. Have feed waiting in the stall, and let him have a couple of mouthfuls before you start to tack him up. Once the animal realizes that the sooner he comes the sooner he is fed, you will have a horse trotting in at your first whistle.

Call him in if the sun is hot, the flies are biting, or if there's a cold wind blowing. Have a carrot and some hay waiting for him, and let him relax a little in his stall before you get him ready to ride. Always make the situation pleasant and desirable so he will want to come in when you call.

Try bringing your horse in after he's been out for a while, even if you don't plan to ride. Give him a carrot, then let him back out. If only good experiences are associated with coming to you, he won't mind being called and brought into his stall.

If your horse attempts to bully you by turning his rump toward you when you enter the stall, encourage him to face you by standing in the doorway and offering a handful of grain or other tidbit. When he reaches for it, let him eat and then calmly put his halter on. If he whirls away before you can put the halter on, try the maneuver again. This time put the lead rope around his neck just behind the ears. Put his halter on after you have control of him with the lead rope.

Encourage him to face and meet you other times by just standing and talking to him in the doorway. When he finally comes over to you, give him a pat or a scratch and leave him to think about it.

In the horse world there is rarely only one way to do something. What works with one horse may not work with another. If your horse's manners have not improved after a reasonable length of time, try a different method of correction. Sometimes a bad habit has been so ingrained by a previous owner that it will never be forgotten by the horse. Either you have to learn to live with it or you will have to sell your horse. Patience, stick-to-itiveness, and time often work wonders with a bad-mannered horse.

TRAILERING

Someday you may have to van your horse to another destination, whether it is to a horse show, another place to trail ride, a friend's barn, or a new home. If you have a horse that loads easily and rides contentedly and calmly, you won't have any problem.

However, if your horse is afraid of or unaccustomed to a trailer, start making it familiar to him slowly, well in advance of moving day. Nothing is more frustrating than being all ready to leave and having a horse who refuses to get in the trailer. Experienced horsemen use various methods to get a frightened or stubborn horse into a trailer, but many are not for the novice backyard horse owner to try.

If you have your own trailer, park it with its doors open and the ramp down in the horse's field so the animal can inspect it at his leisure. The ground around the van should have good footing. Keep it hitched to the vehicle that tows it so it doesn't move or pop up in front when the horse puts his weight on the back of it. Place his hay on the ramp, and each day move the hay a little farther up into the van so the horse has to step onto the ramp and, finally, up into the trailer to reach it.

The van should be a sturdy, safe one—not an open truck or homemade trailer with too steep a ramp. Make sure there is plenty of headroom, and don't try to squeeze a large horse into a too small trailer. Matting or bedding should be put on a smooth trailer floor for better footing. The van should be checked regularly by an experienced mechanic to meet all state regulations, especially with regard to more than adequate brake and taillights. Before driving, check all connections (lights, brakes, hitch, and safety chains) to make sure they are working properly, and that all doors close securely. Check everything again whenever you begin another trip.

Protect your horse's legs and feet with shipping bandages while he is being trailered. Use plenty of padding under the bandage, and cover the legs from the knee down to well over the top of the hoof.

Easier and faster to use are the Velcro-fastened, quilted shipping boots, one for each leg. They cost from $17 to over $100 for four and are well worth it if you have to do much trailering. Don't buy the cheapest you can find. They may not give the necessary protection and will be a waste of money.

Tail wraps are good for horses that sit on the tail gate and rub their tails. They're especially good if you've just spent an hour braiding the tail and don't want the braiding rubbed out by the time you reach a horse show. A tail wrap with Velcro closure costs between $7 and $15.

When loading, talk to your horse and lead him in smoothly, not too fast nor too slow, straight up the ramp. Don't walk him too close to the edge so his feet slip off. Be sure and start your entrance far enough back from the trailer so the horse has a straight shot at it. Horses don't like to round the corner of the trailer and have to step right onto the ramp. Give your animal time to see everything as he is walking toward it.

Position the trailer so that the sun is at your horse's back, shining into the trailer, so the animal isn't walking into a dark, cavelike structure that may be scary. Open the doors in front so he can see outside immediately. A full hay net or manger waiting or a carrot or other treat will make his loading even more enjoyable. The object is to make the trailer so inviting that he will want to walk right in without hesitation.

If you are trailering only one horse, put the animal on the driver's side of the van. The crown of a road is higher than the edge, and this traveling arrangement will balance the trailer better and lessen the chance of its tipping over.

Loading a trailer should be done by two persons, unless your horse is trained to walk into the trailer alone. Don't get in front of the horse while leading him in. Instead, walk into one side of the centrally divided, two-horse trailer and lead your horse into the other. This procedure is to keep you from being trampled, in case something startles him and he jumps forward.

Avoid rushing or pulling. The horse is much stronger than you, and one unhappy incident will make the animal wary of any trailer forever. For a hesitant horse, have two assistants (out of range of a sudden kick) hold a rope across the rump, even with the base of the horse's tailbone, and gently push the horse forward. In the meantime, you should offer encouragement with some oats.

As soon as the animal is in place, immediately snap the trailer chain behind him and close the door or tailgate so the horse can't fly out backward, breaking the chain or going under it. Then tie the horse with a quick-release knot, and reward him with a handful of grain or a carrot. Always

If you are trailering only one horse, put him on the driver's side of the trailer.

stand to one side of a horse, never directly behind or in front. Otherwise, you could be in his path if he decides to bolt forward or backward.

A horse that is more stubborn than afraid can be first threatened, then whacked, on the rump with the bristle end of a broom to persuade him to step lively. Stay out of range of a sudden kick when doing this. A frightened horse may show the whites of his eyes and break out in a sweat, while a stubborn one will appear determined and attempt to bully you.

If you are trailering two horses, put the bigger or heavier one in the stall behind the driver. Load the experienced, calmer one first to reassure the other horse.

Make your horse's first ride a short, slow one with a competent driver and with as little fuss and as few other people involved as possible. Try to arrange the feeding schedule so your horse is not full of feed and water and thus more apt to suffer from motion sickness.

For safety reasons, it is against the law for anyone to ride in the van with a horse. A driver should never travel over 50 miles per hour. He should keep double or triple the length of the van between his vehicle and the one in front. Sudden stops and starts and sharp turns may cause a horse to lose his footing. This problem can be avoided by defensive driving, looking far ahead to avoid emergencies. Try to imagine standing up in the back of a weaving, jouncing trailer without holding on to anything, and you will have some idea what your horse is experiencing.

A horse that has trouble keeping on his feet while riding alone in a trailer can be helped if you remove or tie the center partition to one side. This way he will have more room to spread his feet for better balance.

To unload, untie your horse and toss the lead rope over his neck. Let the ramp down and unhook the tail chain. Start him back out by putting your hand on his chest and give the command, "Back." Have someone at the back of the trailer guide the horse down the ramp where he or she can grab the lead rope.

If you have an experienced horse and you are by yourself, you can untie him, toss the lead rope over his neck, and go around to the back of the trailer. Let the ramp down and undo the tail chain. Then, stand to one side, give a gentle tug on his tail, and say, "Back." As the horse backs out, grab the lead rope when he goes by you.

The more experience your horse has trailering, the easier he will be to load and unload. Always remember to make his trips as pleasant as possible.

Horse Sense on the Trails

Trail riding for most of today's backyard horse owners frequently becomes a jog down public roads, around farmers' fields, and along neighbors' lawns. But whether your ride is through the heavily developed areas of suburbia or through the woods and meadows of a more rural countryside, common sense and common courtesy are necessary for your own and your horse's safety and for continued permission to ride on private property.

PLAN AHEAD

Before participating in a trail ride—whether an all-day outing or just an hour's trot around the block—take into consideration your ability to ride and the condition of both yourself and your horse. To prepare for longer, more strenuous trips, work yourself and your horse into shape with shorter jaunts (about an hour) at first. Gradually lengthen the time of your rides to a couple of hours and quicken your pace. Although the actual ride may not be tiring, especially if your horse is walking most of the time, for the next couple of days afterward you will feel muscles you never knew you had—and so will your horse, if he's not in shape.

Know your horse and his habits or peculiarities. If your mount tends to shy at rotting stumps and protruding boulders or simply at the hollow sound of his own hoofbeats on a wooden bridge, be prepared as you pass by or over one of these "scary monsters." A sudden side jump or 180-degree reverse may cause you to lose your balance and your seat. However, don't overreact to an approaching situation or you will signal your nervousness to your horse. Your horse's mood on the day of your ride will also signal to you how brave or how timid he will be when encountering nature's wonders and man's inventions. He will be a different animal on a hot, humid summer day than on a crisp autumn day with a stiff breeze blowing under his tail.

Your tack and your horse should be inspected before you start out on a trail ride. A broken saddle girth or a thrown shoe can mean a long walk home.

Spray your horse with fly repellent before taking a summer ride. Avoid getting the spray in his eyes. Instead, spray the repellent on an old towel and wipe his face and ears with it. The liquid will discourage the mosquitoes, horseflies, and deerflies (at least for a while). To eliminate extra leather cleaning, do not get any of the repellent on your saddle or other tack.

To make cleaning your horse much easier after a ride on muddy trails, tie long or light-colored tails into a mud knot

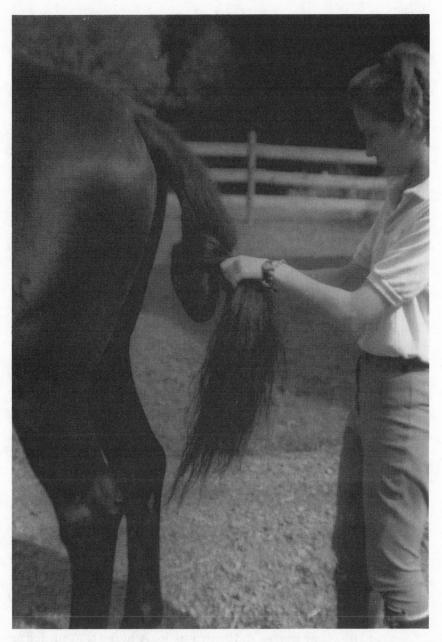

Tie a long or light-colored tail into a mud knot before riding on muddy trails.

by braiding the strands, twisting them into a knot, and fastening them with yarn or cord. This knot will also eliminate much of the staining that yellow or red clay and just plain dirt can do to a white, cream, or gray tail. Unlike the precise tail braiding on a hunter before a show or a fox hunt, the mud knot is not meant to be a thing of beauty, but a creation of convenience. Any intertwining that will stay in place the length of your ride will do.

Remember to clean your horse thoroughly before saddling and bridling him. Even a few grains of caked mud under the saddle can cause a painful sore. Make sure the saddle pad is smooth, because wrinkles in it can also rub your horse's back raw. Tighten the girth by degrees rather than with a sudden jerk, checking to see that it is sufficiently secured before you mount. Nothing is quite as embarrassing as trying to mount and landing on your backside when the saddle slips around and under the horse's belly.

As you learned in your riding lessons, mounting should not be done in the barn or near a fence. A cracked head or slashed leg may be the result of poor distance judging. To spare the horse's back, mount easily and lightly, lowering yourself into the saddle gently, not with a thud.

OUT ON THE TRAILS

Most riding is done in a single file because trails are usually not wide enough for more than one horse. The lead horse should be trailwise and aggressive. A fearful animal will be a problem if he must be the first to walk through streams and past unfamiliar objects. A horse will generally do whatever the other horses in the group do. A horse that jumps or bolts at every movement in the underbrush will be an unsuitable leader because the horses behind will imitate every move, jumping or bolting too.

Horses that tend to kick should be last in line. Many owners tie a red ribbon to a kicker's tail to warn other riders to keep their distance. If you see a red ribbon on a horse's tail in your group, stay well away from him. A horse's kick can reach out much farther than you may think, so to play it safe so you and your horse don't get hurt, leave more distance than you think necessary.

Oldtimers often say, "Walk your horse the first half mile out and the last mile in." This is good advice: Your horse

Check your girth after you mount.

may be stiff after standing for hours in a stall, and the slower pace will give him a chance to loosen up. The end of that first half mile is also a good time to stop and check your girth. Always keep your feet in the stirrups when you tighten the girth. This is a safety precaution, in case your horse bolts or shies at something.

Whether you are walking along a heavily traveled highway, cantering down a path through an overgrown field, or maneuvering a steep, rocky trail through dense woods, the most important rule is to have your mount under control at all times. In some circumstances, an experienced horse knows how to handle obstacles better than an experienced rider. At such moments, loosen your reins and give your mount his head, but be prepared to gather up the reins quickly. A pheasant may suddenly fly up in his face, and steady reins will be needed to calm him.

GROUND SURFACES—WHEN TO WALK, TROT, OR CANTER

Various ground surfaces can cause problems for trail riders. Mud holes and boggy areas should be avoided whenever possible. If you must travel through them, walk your horse. Mud is very slippery, and can create suction that can even pull a shoe off. Boggy areas in which you think your horse might sink should be tested first. Dismount and step onto the surface yourself to determine how deep your horse may go down. Remount and start across slowly. If, as you progress through the bog, he starts to panic or scramble wildly, try to keep him calm: Halt, reassure him, and then start again slowly so he doesn't pull a muscle.

If freezing is predicted later in the day or evening, the ruts made by your horse's hooves will harden into uneven footing, rough going for horses on succeeding days, and another reason to avoid muddy areas on trails.

Snow, too, deserves respect. Hard balls of ice can build up in your horse's feet and make it seem as though the animal is on ice skates. Walking on ice-caked hooves through snow and over ice gives a horse very little traction. You can get off periodically and knock out the snow balls, but it is safer not to ride in these circumstances.

Horses without shoes should be kept off hard surfaces, or their feet will soon become tender and sore. Roadways of gravel and small stones may also be hazardous, because pebbles can get stuck in a horse's foot and cause painful bruises. (Horses seldom ridden are sometimes left unshod to save on expenses. Shoes are not necessary for horses rarely worked unless there is a hoof problem.)

Even if your horse is shod, travel at a walk or slow trot on paved roads. The hard surface can inflict many kinds of leg and foot ailments. Unless a horse has borium on his shoes (similar to studs on a car's tires), paved roads can be almost as slippery as ice because of the oil deposited on them by cars. If you think there is a chance that your horse might fall, remove your feet from the stirrups so that you can jump free if he starts to go down.

Riding on heavily traveled roads should be avoided, but, if it is necessary, ride in a single file on the right-hand side of the road as far from the traffic as possible. Some riders prefer the left-hand side, as pedestrians do, so that their horses can see the oncoming traffic. However, this is not recommended: It is much more frightening for a horse to see a large truck roaring right toward him. And if he shies suddenly he could toss his rider right into the truck's path.

If your horse is apprehensive about an approaching vehicle, turn to face it as it passes. Do this in a driveway or wider area along the road, so you both are away from oncoming traffic. A horse facing the frightening object from a distance will be less likely to bolt.

In many areas horses still have the right-of-way, but since there are more cars than horses, challenging vehicles in the middle of a busy intersection is not advisable. Always look before crossing a road, be it country lane or interstate highway.

Be twice as cautious if you are riding along a road at night. Wear light-colored clothes and put reflecting tape on the back of your saddle and on your horse's tail. If your horse will tolerate it, cut a piece of white sheet to drape over his hindquarters. Stick reflecting tape on it and attach it to the cantle of your saddle for added protection.

Wave down speeding motorists so that they slow up when passing, and always thank considerate drivers.

Cantering or galloping across a strange field is foolhardy if you don't keep a sharp lookout. An unexpected hole dug by a groundhog, mole, or other small animal may cause serious injuries to both you and your horse if your mount steps into it. Watch for mounds of soft dirt, for they often signal the existence of such holes. Be wary when crossing through a hedgerow or going through a fence that is down. Barbed wire and postholes are often hidden by heavy brush.

Before taking an unfamiliar jump, check the footing and clearance on the other side. Don't jump while trail riding alone if you and your horse lack experience and training. A phone and help may be too far away if you fall and injure yourself.

Watch for bottles, cans, and broken glass discarded by our "throwaway society," because they can give your horse a nasty cut. Warn the riders behind you to prevent their horses from stepping on them, too.

Streams and puddles mean different things to different horses. To some they look inviting, while to others they are terrifying. Either way, make your horse walk through them. Don't allow him to jump, or he may end up on the heels of the horses in front of him or sink up to his knees in mud on the opposite bank.

If your horse stops in midstream and wants to take a drink, you may allow a few sips if you're sure the water is not polluted and if the horse isn't overheated. However, if he begins to paw, kick him on, for pawing is often a signal that he is planning to lie down and roll.

If your horse is frightened of the water and starts to balk, try to keep him moving, but do so gently and firmly, reassuring him repeatedly. Don't tense up or try to force him into the water, as this will only cause more fright. A sniff and a few sips may help convince your horse that this liquid is just like the water in his bucket back home.

The reasoning behind a horse's fear dates back to his wild ancestors. Instinct tells horses to take very good care of their feet and legs because if one or the other is injured, the horse can't walk. In the wild he then has no protection and is easy prey to many other wild animals. A river or a stream where he can't see the bottom or isn't sure what the bottom is will therefore be of great concern to him. Mud is a danger to his legs.

If the stream is narrow enough, your horse may leap across from a standstill, so be prepared to hang on to his mane rather than the reins so you don't jerk him in the mouth. It's better for your horse to walk calmly rather than to leap wildly, but this may take time and practice to correct.

If your horse absolutely refuses to cross a stream don't try to lead him across. It won't work. Tugging on his mouth is less convincing than driving him forward with your legs. And, in addition to getting your feet wet, if he does decide to follow you, you may have a thousand pounds land on you. A horse will often follow you by trying to be on the same spot that you are, and at the same time! He feels that if it's safe for you to stand there, then it must be safe for him to stand there, too. A much better solution is to have a trail-experienced horse go first, your horse following right behind.

While you are crossing, watch out for floating branches that may strike against and twist between your horse's legs. Feeling much like snakes, the branches may prompt a leap forward and perhaps a slip on moss-covered rocks, giving you an unexpected dunking.

When meeting steep banks, your horse will be able to jump up or down those that rise less than 3 feet or half his height. A gradual slope may be climbed or slid down. On a decline, always walk your horse to avoid slipping down against the horse in front. Your mount's body should be straight, hindquarters in line with forehead. Push your feet just far enough in front of you so that the stirrup leathers remain vertical to the ground. Keep the reins loose, allowing the horse freedom of head and neck. Do not try to hold him up.

Going uphill, lean forward, standing up out of the saddle so that your weight is over the horse's shoulders. Grab the mane to pull yourself up and to help maintain your balance. This technique keeps your weight off the horse's hindquarters so he can use them to push off.

When trotting downhill, don't attempt to post, but instead stand slightly in your stirrups. It's easier on you and the horse. For long canters or gallops, again stand slightly in your stirrups, leaning a little forward in the "half-seat" position. This hand-gallop position is not so tiring as sitting down in the saddle and will conserve your energy and your horse's.

If you must ride through a heavily developed area, be ready for anything. A door opening suddenly, a barking dog, or a flapping sheet on a clothesline can unnerve even the steadiest, quietest horse.

POLITENESS COUNTS

Trail-riding manners should always be practiced for your own and your fellow riders' safety. Use hand or voice signals to warn those behind you of any change in gait. Never ride too close to the horse in front of you; the animal may become irritated and kick you or your mount, possibly unseating his own rider at the same time.

If you are in line with other riders, don't allow your horse to push past the others to get in front. If you are walking, this can be very irritating to other riders, but if you are moving on at a faster pace, it could also be dangerous. Some horses will take this restraint as a challenge and will go faster to the point of getting out of control if they think another horse is trying to pass them.

If you are first in line, keep your pace steady. Don't allow your horse to trot off whenever he wants or to stop suddenly so the horses behind all bump into each other.

Don't try to hold branches out of the way of the rider behind you. Your arms aren't long enough to hold them until the next rider can reach them. Just push through the branches and try as best as you can not to let them snap back into another rider's or his horse's face.

If you plan on riding through private property, permission should first be obtained. Consideration should be shown toward the owners of the land over which you are riding. Always close any gates that you open to pass through. No farmer or rancher will appreciate having to round up loose cattle or other animals.

Think of these landowners, too, by not scaring their livestock or riding through their cultivated fields. A horse's hooves can chop down young plants, ruining a large portion of the crops. Even when riding along the edge of a cultivated field, make sure the ground isn't muddy and you aren't leaving holes or kicking up great clods of earth wherever your horse walks. When a farmer rides through on his tractor, he doesn't want to be jouncing from one rut to the next.

Keep to the trails so that you don't trample wildflowers, delicate ground cover, lawns, or gardens. Remember that you and your horse are guests on someone else's property. Careless destruction will cause generous owners to close their land to horses and riders.

A PAUSE BY THE WAYSIDE

Stopping for lunch or a break may be necessary and welcome to all those taking part in a long trail ride. Upon dismounting, loosen your horse's girth. If you have an English saddle, run your stirrups up the leathers, tucking the ends of the leathers through the stirrups to secure them in place. Tether your horse by a halter or a neck rope, never by the bridle. One good jerk can easily break it, resulting in costly repairs and damage to your horse's mouth.

Be sure your mount is cooled down. Never let a hot horse stand or drink water.

Tie your horse's halter rope to a branch above his head or with the rope short enough so that he can't get his head

Tether your horse by a halter or neck rope—never by the bridle, as one good jerk can easily break it.

down and a front foot hooked over the rope. Use a knot that can be untied quickly in an emergency. Separate the horses so that they cannot kick or bite each other. If you leave the bridle on, loop the reins behind the raised stirrups so that the reins are out of the horse's way. Tie the horses where you can see them, so that any problems can be noticed immediately.

Before leaving the picnic area, clean up your rubbish and dispose of it in receptacles or, if none are available, take it home with you. Extinguish your campfire completely with water, dirt, or sand.

See that girths are tightened and bridles on correctly before you resume your ride.

HOME AGAIN

As you near the barn, keep your horse at a walk, even though he may want to pick up his pace. Galloping home is an easy way to lose control of your mount and to receive a good crack on the head as the horse charges into a low-beamed barn. Walking the last mile home is also an excellent way of cooling your horse off without having to do a lot of walking around on foot later.

Give your horse a good rubdown after a long trail ride, checking for any soreness, heat, or sores on his back, legs, and feet. If you find anything unusual, treat it accordingly. (See chapter 9.)

Common sense and courtesy combined with a little "horse sense" should guarantee you many pleasant days of trail riding. One last bit of advice deserves repeating: Stay alert, and always expect the unexpected when trail riding.

Is There a Horse Doctor in the House?

Even the healthiest horses get sick, but to lessen the chances of its happening to your horse, practice preventive measures—regular inoculations and worming as well as daily grooming, feeding, and barn cleaning.

Conscientious care is a lot easier and less expensive than having to nurse a horse back to good health. Not being able to ride because the horse is getting over an injury or illness is also a nuisance.

As soon as you buy a horse, a preventive medical program should be set up with your veterinarian. It should include vaccinations for influenza and encephalomyelitis (sleeping sickness), a permanent tetanus immunization with annual boosters, a Coggins test for equine infectious anemia, and wormings (four to six times a year). In some areas vaccinations for rabies, botulism, and Potomac fever (see later in this chapter) are also recommended. There is

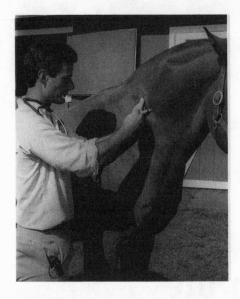

Regular inoculations are good preventative measures to help keep your horse healthy.

the real possibility that neglect in planning such a program could cause the animal's death.

Although a veterinarian should be called promptly at the first sign of difficulty—listlessness, coughing, unusual lumps or swellings, pacing as if in pain, runny nose and eyes, diarrhea or constipation, heat in the legs or feet, an open wound, or lack of interest in food—there are treatments for minor ills and injuries that every horse-owning family should know. To be able to perform this type of first aid, you must have in your horse's medicine cabinet:

A blunt-ended veterinary rectal thermometer

Sterile cotton and gauze bandages

Antiseptic dusting powder

Epsom salts

Surgical soap

Liniment

Colic remedy

Worm medicine

Boric acid powder

Petroleum jelly

Iodine (tincture of)

Methylene blue

Blunt-ended scissors

Vetrap

Rubbing alcohol

Topical ointment

A dose syringe for liquid medicine

Many of these items can be acquired as you need them. In time, your cabinet will be overflowing with lotions, powders, and ointments. Be sure to use only those your veterinarian recommends for a particular illness or injury. The wrong medicine may lead to serious complications.

Bring all medicines into your house during the winter so that they do not freeze.

FIRST AID

Every horse is an individual, just as each person is. What one horse does may be perfectly normal for him, but for another the same behavior may be the first stage of some illness. Know your horse so you can determine whether that afternoon nap, half-eaten feed, or loose bowel movement is typical or whether it means trouble.

The average number of bowel movements of an average healthy horse is eight each day, but, like all estimates, this will depend on the individual horse.

The normal temperature for a horse is from 99.5 degrees to 100.5 degrees Fahrenheit (37.5 to 38.1 Celsius). One hundred and three degrees Fahrenheit (41.1 Celsius) is entering the danger zone. Take your horse's temperature a couple of times at different times of the day when he is healthy so you will have a comparison.

If you think your horse has a high temperature, check with the veterinarian promptly.

Puncture Wounds

Puncture wounds, such as those caused by a nail, should be washed clean with warm water and antibacterial soap, and opened so they will drain. A soft stream of water from a hose will help flush out any debris. Bleeding will also help to clean the wound. If your horse has not already received his annual tetanus shot, call your vet immediately.

Puncture wounds are very dangerous because you only see the tip of the iceberg, especially in tendon areas. They can even lead to death.

Abrasions

Abrasions, such as those caused by rubbing the tail during shipping, should be smeared with petroleum jelly. Saddle and girth sores require being painted with methylene blue several times daily. No riding should be allowed until these are completely healed.

Rope burns usually respond to methylene blue. You should try to get them to heal without a scab if they are located below the fetlock, because the scabs will crack open whenever the horse moves.

Cuts

Cuts from barbed wire, glass, or other objects should be cleaned and a topical ointment applied if you are sure suturing is not necessary (call your vet if the bleeding is severe and you think suturing is required). While waiting, flush out any debris with a stream of water. You may have to use a soft brush to get out shards of glass or dirt. Bleeding will help clean the wound, but if it is profuse you will have to apply pressure to the wound to stop the bleeding until the vet arrives.

If a leg artery is slashed, the blood (bright red in color) will spurt and you must use direct pressure to slow or stop it. If the slashed artery is on the body, apply pressure between the wound and the heart, feeling around until you find the place that reduces the flow best. If a vein is cut, the blood (dark red in color) will flow or ooze, and you must apply pressure on the side of the wound away from the heart. Do not use a tourniquet.

Cold compresses will slow down the bloodflow of minor wounds, but do not cover a bleeding wound immediately, because the flow will wash away any germs. Infection sets in easily, so watch the wound and surrounding area for danger signs: swelling, soreness, excessive heat, and, a few days later, a pus discharge.

COMMON AILMENTS

The most common horse ailments are colic, the common cold, flu, respiratory diseases, and lameness. You should be able to recognize their symptoms, know when to call your veterinarian, and be able to help your horse until the vet arrives.

Colic

Colic refers to abdominal pain produced by various abnormal conditions, such as gas, a sudden twist of the intestine, or an impaction (a ball of undigested food blocking the intestine).

The horse's one-way digestive system makes him unable to vomit as a cat or dog does, and anything harmful to him must be rejected through elimination. Because of this system, a horse is particularly susceptible to forage poisoning or botulism, brought about most often by consuming spoiled grain. It can also occur if your horse eats poisonous weeds sometimes found in hay or even lurking in your pasture.

Colic contributes to more deaths in horses than any other single illness. Every colic case is an emergency that requires astute observation and professional assistance.

Cause. Poor feeding procedures such as overfeeding, feeding when the horse is hot or excited, or feeding spoiled or moldy food.

Symptoms. A horse with colic may break out in a sweat, bite or kick at his side, paw the ground, or lie down and roll. However, the degree of pain exhibited is not related to the severity of the colic. Sand colic caused by a buildup of sand in the intestines is deadly, but only causes a gradual onset of dull pain.

Treatment. Call your vet immediately and follow instructions until he or she arrives. You may be told to get your horse on his feet and walk him if he is thrashing and rolling around, because rolling can cause him to twist his intestine. But walk him slowly so you don't exhaust him.

Take away hay and grain, but do allow small amounts of water. Take his temperature, pulse, and respiration rate every thirty minutes and write down your findings. Also record any other observations such as obvious pain bouts or anxiety attacks. If the horse is not inflicting damage on himself, let him stand or lie quietly, and keep him warm with blankets.

Coughs and Colds

Coughs and colds, to which young horses are particularly susceptible, are similar to those in people.

Symptoms. Nasal discharge, nagging cough, high temperature, lack of appetite, and spiritlessness.

Treatment. Keep your horse warm and well blanketed. Feed a hot bran mash (see chapter 5) once a day, allow plenty of rest, and give whatever medication your vet prescribes. Colds are contagious, so isolate your horse from others for the ten to fourteen days of the illness.

Prevention. Do not put your horse away hot. Cool him off thoroughly after riding. Do not leave him standing in drafts, or allow him to get overtired or chilled.

Equine Influenza

Equine influenza, or the flu, is contracted usually by young animals but is rarely fatal.

Symptoms. A high temperature (as much as 106 degrees Fahrenheit, 41.1 Celsius, for two to ten days), loss of appetite, weakness, rapid breathing, a dry cough, and a watery discharge from eyes and nostrils.

Treatment. Isolation and rest are recommended until the temperature and cough diminish.

Prevention. Your horse should be vaccinated about a month before he comes into contact with other horses, such as at a horse show. Usually two injections are given two to four weeks apart, and then an annual booster.

Shipping Fever

Shipping fever, also known as distemper or strangles, is a highly contagious upper respiratory disease caused by bacteria streptococcus equi (strep equi).

Symptoms. A high temperature and loss of appetite, followed by a nasal discharge and a swelling and probable abscessing of the lymph nodes under the jaw. The infection runs its course in two to four weeks.

Treatment. Your veterinarian, who will usually treat the bacteria with antibiotics, will tell you how to deal with any abscesses. Your horse should be isolated, if possible, given complete rest, fresh drinking water, and light feeds like bran mashes. He should be kept out of drafts.

Lameness

Lameness is caused by many things ranging from an injury to overwork without proper conditioning to thrush to navicular disease. (See "Diseases" later in this chapter.) Some problems are more serious than others and they all have their own treatments.

A stone lodged in the foot, overwork, bad shoeing, strains, bruises, infection, scratches, navicular disease, abscesses, and splints can all be sources of lameness. Your horse should not be ridden until the condition is pinpointed and corrected.

Determine which leg is affected by trotting the horse on hard ground. He will raise his head when the bad foot goes down to take weight off the injured leg, usually a front one. Clean out the sore foot to see if there is a stone, nail, or piece of glass causing the trouble.

If your horse has been shod within the last three days, you should have the shoe removed from the lame leg. A poorly placed nail may be causing the lameness, or an abscess may have formed at a place other than where a nail is. Inappropriate trimming or shoeing can aggravate and even cause lameness involving the foot and pastern.

Foot abscesses may also be caused by gravel or dirt entering sensitive parts of the foot due to cracks in the foot. Place your hands around the problem hoof and compare it with the opposite foot to feel whether there is any heat in the wall of the problem hoof. An abscess will cause severe lameness and heat in the foot.

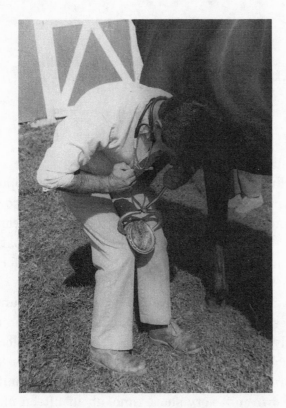

If your horse is lame, your vet may use hoof testers to see if the problem is in the foot.

If you feel heat in the foot, soak it in hot water with epsom salts and poultice it. (Use a commercial poultice, such as Uptite, and spread the white claylike material thickly on the bottom of the sore foot. Cut a piece of paper bag in the shape of the hoof and lay it over the poultice, wrapping Vetrap and then duct tape around it to hold it in place. Make sure there is no pressure on the coronary band of the hoof.) Consult with your veterinarian if there is no improvement in forty-eight hours.

If the problem doesn't appear to be in the foot, go over the leg, working down from the elbow and looking for heat, swelling, or tenderness. If there is nothing that you can see, then the trouble may be in the shoulder or the stifle. Call your veterinarian for diagnosis and recommended treatment.

OTHER PROBLEMS

Choking

Choking is related to the horse's eating habits.

Cause. A lump of food gets stuck in the horse's esophagus. Saliva is produced but the horse can't get his feed down so he drools excessively. Feed mixed with saliva may come out of his nostrils. A horse overdue to have his teeth floated (see "Teeth" in this chapter) is a prime candidate for a choke episode because he can't chew his food properly.

Treatment. Call your vet. Keep your horse calm until the vet arrives by walking him or standing with him and talking quietly. Massage the throat area to push the blockage down. Choking is an emergency, but not a disaster because the horse can still breathe. Most episodes usually pass on their own in a very short time, about fifteen minutes.

Prevention. Feed hay before grain so the horse is full and less likely to bolt his grain. Place *large* rocks in the grain bucket, which will force the horse to slow down and pick his way around the rocks to eat his grain.

Cracked Heels

Cracked heels are similar to the chapped hands of a human and occur in the hollow of the pastern, not the heel.

Cause. Standing for long periods in soaking wet pastures and mud. Also when the legs are washed repeatedly and not dried properly.

Symptoms. Scaling and scabbing that produce painful cracks and will become infected if not treated promptly.

Treatment. Wash well with soap and water to remove all loose matter. Dry *very* thoroughly and apply either petroleum jelly or an antiseptic ointment.

Prevention. When your horse is out on wet, muddy pastures, smear petroleum jelly two times a week over the hollow of the pastern.

Itchy Tail

Itchy tail is a common condition in horses and ponies of all ages, particularly in the summer.

Cause. Mange mites, pinworms, fungi, and allergic reactions from biting insects.

Symptoms. Rubbing the base of his tail on walls, doorways, and gateposts until the area becomes inflamed and raw, and the hair is rubbed away.

Treatment. If you are on a good worming program ask your vet to examine the area for mange mites. He may recommend worming the horse if it hasn't been done recently and treating with a fungicide, an insecticide, and then a fungicide again over a period of six to eight days.

Prevention. If your horse has an allergy to biting insects you will have to practice good stable management to keep insects at a minimum and try to keep the horse away from them.

Melanoma

Melanoma is a small growth (tumor) that is frequently found in gray or white horses. It may or may not be malignant and should be examined by your vet, who will probably tell you to ignore it since most melanomas are only cosmetic and surgery may cause them to spread.

Symptoms. Small, hard lumps develop around the anus and tail base. They may continue to spread internally. Persistent lameness in the hind leg or legs of a gray or white horse should alert the owner to the possibility of an internal malignant melanoma.

Treatment. There is none. When the growths are external and causing no discomfort or lameness, they should be left alone. If they become malignant, most horses are humanely destroyed.

Rain Rot

Rain rot is a skin disease caused by a funguslike organism that normally lives in the soil and is present in dust particles. It multiplies rapidly on the horse's skin, where it mixes with skin secretions and dandruff.

Symptoms. Hard, painful scabs cemented to the horse's skin. They appear during late summer or early fall after a period of rain that has followed a dry, dusty spell. The dusty conditions preceding the rain fill the horse's coat and cover his skin with the fungus-laden dust particles. Then the rain brings the moisture that encourages the organism to multiply and infect the horse's skin.

Treatment. Use a mild dandruff shampoo or a good antiseptic pet shampoo and thoroughly clean the skin. Massage the skin as you wash it, gently working the scabs loose. Treat the affected areas with ichthamol salve and keep the horse out of the rain. If not treated, the infection will cause most of the hair in the crusted areas to fall out.

Prevention. Regular grooming to get as much dirt as possible out of the horse's coat, and a bath twice a month with a good pet shampoo.

Ringworm

Ringworm is a very contagious disease.

Cause. Several different fungal organisms that an infected horse passes on to another horse through direct contact.

Symptoms. Hair will fall out, leaving circular bald areas.

Treatment. An infected horse should be isolated. All grooming equipment must be disinfected with an iodine preparation and used only on that horse. Lesions should be dressed once a week for three weeks using an antifungal application. Always wear rubber gloves when grooming the infected horse because ringworm is infectious to humans, too.

Splints

Splints are unsightly bony enlargements on a horse's lower leg. When the bone-forming cells in the bone lining are stimulated by injury, they grow new bone, creating an enlargement on the existing bone. Splints form on the cannon bone where the splint bone attaches, usually on the inside of the front legs, a little below the knee.

Cause. Stimulation of the bone-forming cells from the strain of hard training, injury, poor conformation, and concussion.

Splints usually occur in horses under five years of age. Heat, pain, and swelling may occur, but the pain and lameness will subside in two or three weeks. The swelling will become harder as the inflammatory fluid and tissue change into bone.

Treatment. No riding until the horse trots off without

any sign of lameness. DMSO (a liquid that is used to carry an anti-inflammatory or an analgesic) may be rubbed on the area to try to reduce the size of the splint.

Summer Sores

Summer sores are the result of any cut or wound in which a parasitic infection creates a chronic skin condition.

Cause. Flies often carry eggs of small white worms, which mature into larvae inside the fly's body. These larvae are deposited by flies in the open wounds of horses; the larvae then burrow down into the horse's flesh.

Symptoms. Inflammation, swelling, itchy lumps, and, often, raw spots that may ooze pus.

Treatment. Kill the worm larvae with medication.

Prevention. Wounds should be protected so that flies can't get at them. Fly control and use of the drug ivermectin as a dewormer can prevent summer sores.

Swellings

Swellings are lumps in soft tissue.

Cause. They may be caused by an injection if either the medication didn't disperse properly or some infectious agent was introduced with the needle. They may also be caused by insect bites, allergies, or minor injuries.

Treatment. If the swelling is in the same area as the injection, take your horse's temperature. If there is no fever then it is probably not an infection. Increase the circulation to the area to disperse the medicine by applying hot soaks, DMSO, and a little massage. Check the lump for a day or two to see how it is doing.

Treat other lumps with cold hosing for a couple of days. Cold should be applied for the first forty-eight to seventy-two hours. Then heat therapy can begin with hot towels, hot water bottles, or immersion in warm water a minimum of fifteen to twenty-five minutes, three to four times a day. A good way to remember when to apply cold or hot treatments is "Cold today, hot tamale."

Worms

Almost all animals have some worms, and horses have several different kinds, which, if kept in check by regular wormings, are not necessarily harmful. Like all parasites, however, worms do live at the expense of their host, and a horse's condition will deteriorate if their numbers are allowed to multiply.

If not treated promptly, a horse heavily infested with worms will die. Even after they're removed, worms may cause colic because of the permanent but unseen damage done to the intestines.

Symptoms. Loss of weight (in spite of a good appetite), a dull coat, constant tail rubbing, a listless attitude, and generally unhealthy appearance. In addition to roundworms, pinworms, and bloodworms (the most dangerous), there is another common internal parasite—the larva of the horse botfly.

The female fly lays her eggs on the horse's legs and underside of his body, where he can reach them with his mouth. The yellow eggs are found in clusters attached to the hair and can be removed by scraping (pick up a botfly scraper at your local tack or feed store) or washing away with hot water.

The eggs are licked up by the horse and then hatch,

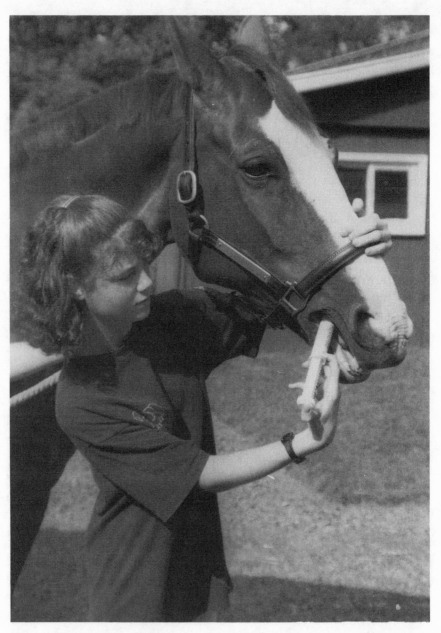

Set up a worming schedule four to six times annually to keep internal worms under control.

penetrating all mucous membranes and causing ulcers in the mouth. They will eventually work their way to the stomach where they attach to the stomach lining.

To prevent or control parasites in your barn, you should provide your horse with a clean stall, sanitary feed and water containers, and covered feed bins. Outside, you should practice the following:

- Have more than one pasture so you can practice rotation grazing.
- Don't spread fresh manure in grazing fields.
- Pick up droppings in small paddocks.
- Have the manure pile removed regularly.
- Don't allow horses to drink from barnyard puddles or to eat grain or hay from the ground, where manure drainage and worms may contaminate them.
- Avoid overgrazing, because there are more parasites on the bottom inch of grass.
- Keep pastures mowed to destroy the parasites' breeding and growing grounds.
- Send a manure sample to your veterinarian in early spring and late fall, so the variety of worms and the degree of infestation can be determined. Set up a worming schedule with your vet (worm four to six times annually), rotating different medicines so that the worms don't become immune to them.

OTHER HORSE DISEASES

The following partial list of diseases—with their causes, symptoms, treatments, and preventions—is only to supplement the services of your veterinarian and to aid you in recognizing an illness.

Azoturia

Azoturia, also known as "tying up," affects the muscles of the loins and hindquarters.

Cause. Working an out-of-shape horse too hard or over-feeding a well-conditioned horse without giving the usual exercise.

Symptoms. Horse refuses to move forward and breaks out in a sweat; muscles in the hind end become hard.

Treatment. Stop working the horse immediately and keep him warm and quiet, with a blanket over the loins.

Prevention. Warm your horse up gradually. Feed him according to the amount of work he is doing, and exercise him regularly.

Botulism

Botulism is a poisoning resulting from the ingestion of a toxin produced by a certain bacteria. The disease, which attacks the nervous system, is more common in certain areas of the country, such as Kentucky. It is not transmitted from horse to horse.

Symptoms. The horse has difficulty in breathing; he is off his feed, can't drink, and is depressed, sluggish, constipated. Pull out his tongue and he will let it hang out.

Treatment. Botulism is usually fatal. An antitoxin is available but costs between $2,000 and $2,500, and the prognosis is still poor. Death is caused by paralysis to the respiratory system so the horse can't breathe.

Prevention. Vaccination. Keep manure away from barn and pastures so bacteria spores don't run down with rain water into pastures.

Encephalomyelitis

Encephalomyelitis, or sleeping sickness, is caused by viruses that are carried from infected areas to clean ones by mosquitoes and birds. The two most common forms are the Eastern and Western strains. An outbreak of Venezuelan equine encephalomyelitis (VEE) first occurred in Texas in 1971. The Eastern and VEE forms of the disease are almost always fatal. VEE is contagious to humans, too.

Symptoms. Sleepy appearance, wandering aimlessly and without coordination, grinding of teeth, inability to swallow, standing with head down, and even blindness. Infected animals either recover or die in two to four days.

Treatment. A veterinarian should be called at once, because serum is sometimes effective if given early enough. Good nursing, with possible forced feeding and watering, will aid your horse's recovery.

Prevention. Mosquitoes should be controlled by keeping barn and pastures well drained. All horses should be vaccinated before May of each year or when the disease makes its appearance in your area.

Equine Infectious Anemia

Equine infectious anemia, or swamp fever, is an infectious viral disease spread by any bloodsucking insect, particularly stable flies.

Symptoms. High and intermittent fever; stiffness and weakness, especially in the hindquarters; anemia; loss of weight but not loss of appetite; and swelling of the lower body and legs. Most infected animals die within two to four weeks. However, some horses recover, but since they are carriers for the rest of their lives, they should be destroyed to protect other horses.

Prevention. Practice good sanitation to reduce the number of biting insects and have your horse tested annually for infection with a Coggins test, a blood test used to determine whether a horse has equine infectious anemia.

Founder

Founder is an inflammation of the sensitive part of the hoof's interior.

Cause. The disease can be caused by overeating, drinking cold water, improper cooling off after hard exercise, or fast riding on a hard surface that results in injury to the blood vessels of one or more feet (usually the front ones). Access to too much lush spring grass is the biggest cause of founder, which is aggravated by obesity.

A foundered horse will experience intense pain and the affected feet will be hot and sensitive to the touch. The horse's temperature may go as high as 106 degrees Fahrenheit (41.1 Celsius), and the patient will break out in a heavy sweat. The damage to the feet will be permanent, with a wrinkling or series of rings on the front wall of the foot. In fatal conditions, the coffin bone drops through the bottom of the foot.

Treatment. Apply wet cold packs to the feet, or stand the horse in a cool stream until the vet arrives. Special trimming and corrective shoeing will probably be needed after the disease has been brought under control.

Heaves

Heaves, similar to asthma in humans, is an incurable respiratory ailment that comes on very slowly over a long period of time.

Symptoms. A deep, hacking cough, difficulty in breathing, a whistling or wheezing sound when the horse inhales, and shortness of wind. The horse's flanks will heave even after mild exertion, and every attack causes additional damage to the air sacs in the lungs.

Treatment. A horse that develops the heaves must be rested immediately or the condition could be fatal. Avoid dusty hay and dusty trails; wet your hay and grain down. Use a cough medicine prescribed by your vet, who may also tell you to substitute pellet concentrates and other special feeds for hay. Avoid long, hard periods of exercising, and slowly get your horse in condition to be used for nearby trail rides and mild ring work.

Prevention. Good ventilation will help to prevent heaves. With proper care the condition can be relieved if not too far developed.

Navicular Disease

Navicular disease is a disease of the navicular bone, a small bone at the back of the foot. It is most commonly seen in older horses, especially those who have had a fair amount of pounding on their forefeet during their life, such as from roadwork or jumping.

Symptoms. Lameness, usually in both front feet, is the first sign of navicular disease. The horse takes short steps, putting his toes down first in an effort to keep weight off his heels. He will stumble frequently. The vet will X-ray the foot or feet for supporting evidence of navicular disease.

Treatment. If the horse is young and the disease is detected early, corrective shoes and proper exercise may eliminate the symptoms. A neurectomy operation (cutting the nerves that supply sensation to the area) can be a last resort; this operation removes all pain and stops the lameness, but does not cure the disease.

Potomac Horse Fever

Potomac horse fever is a disease first detected in Maryland in 1979. It has traveled from coast to coast, and from Canada to Texas. How it is transmitted is still uncertain. In the same barn one or two horses may get the disease while the rest show no signs of it. It is seen more in certain areas, such as Maryland.

Symptoms. High temperature, severe diarrhea, depression, and poor appetite. The horse will be very sick for days and can die by secondary dehydration in spite of the best treatment.

Treatment. Intensive nursing care, involving fluid therapy and appropriate antibiotics.

Prevention. Vaccinations, sometimes every six months.

Tetanus

Tetanus, or lockjaw, is caused by bacteria that enter the body, usually through a wound. Death occurs in over 50 percent of the cases. Tetanus affects all ages, although it is rarely seen today due to vigilant vaccination programs.

Symptoms. The first sign of the disease is a stiffness about the head. The horse chews slowly and swallows with difficulty. Next, the third or inner eyelid protrudes over the eyeball, and the slightest movement or noise starts violent spasms in the affected horse. Usually the sick horse will continue standing almost until death.

Treatment. Call your vet immediately to give the wounded animal an injection of antiserum, which must be administered within seventy-two hours after the injury. The sick horse should be kept as quiet and as comfortable as possible, with plenty of water and soft feed available.

Prevention. The stable area should be kept clean and tetanus toxoid given in two doses at six-week intervals by your veterinarian. Booster shots should then be given annually.

Thrush

Thrush causes the frog of the hoof to become rotten and soft, and is accompanied by a strong odor of decay. It is caused by little or no care of the hoofs and lack of sanitary conditions in the stall. It can be avoided by keeping the stall clean and by using the hoof pick regularly to remove packed manure from your horse's hooves. The condition needs constant and often prolonged treatment, under the direction of your veterinarian.

TEETH

Teeth are very important to a horse's well-being. Unhealthy, irregular teeth may cause the horse to swallow food whole, so it passes right through the digestive system, or the horse may drop food while chewing. Both may result in problems of nutrition.

All horses wear their teeth down through chewing, but, unlike human teeth, horses' molars keep on growing until the horse is quite old. As the softer cement surfaces of the teeth wear away through constant grinding, sharp points of hard enamel protrude to keep the surface rough for grinding. Sometimes these sharp points poke painfully into the opposite gums or cause sores on the side of the tongue or the inside of the cheek. The horse will not be able to eat without considerable pain. The animal may also object to a bit put in his mouth, constantly champing on it and tossing his head.

To smooth these sharp surfaces, your veterinarian or a horse dentist should check your horse's teeth once or twice a year and, if necessary, "float," or file them down.

BANDAGING

Leg bandages may be used to give support to a leg by reinforcing weak tendons, for protection on a horse that is being vanned to another destination and will be standing for a long period of time, or to cover a wound. Bandages differ in materials used and ways of applying, according to the purpose, but all have some do's and don'ts.

- Do put your horse in crossties before beginning to wrap.
- Don't sit down on the floor but crouch down as you wrap, so you can move out of the way if the horse kicks.
- Don't wrap without first applying a thick layer of cotton for cushioning around the leg.
- Do make the bandage only tight enough to stay in place.
- Don't wrap the bandages so tight that you stop the circulation.
- Do wrap the bandage smoothly, following the contours of the leg.
- Don't wrap over the knee.
- Do start at the top of the area you wish to wrap, work

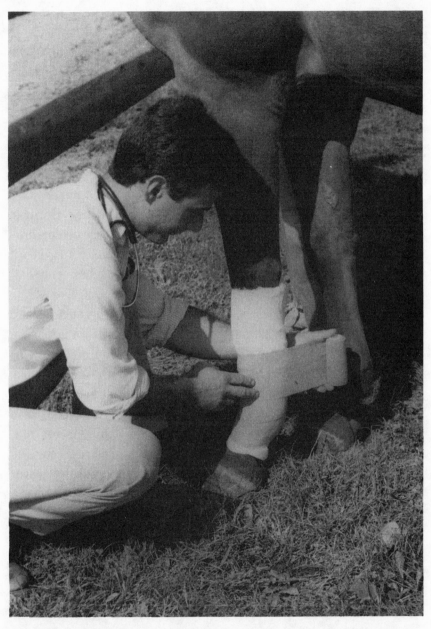

Leg bandages should not be applied without first wrapping a thick layer of cotton for cushioning around the leg.

down, and then back to the top, where you can tie the two ends together in a bow.

- Don't end with a knot that is too difficult to undo quickly.
- Do tie or fasten the bandage on the outside of the leg, not the inside, front or back.

CALLING YOUR VETERINARIAN

Horses can become infected with many of the same diseases that people get—glaucoma, sinusitis, heart failure, rhinitis, and pneumonia, among them. When you call the veterinarian about your sick horse, you should be prepared to give all the information requested, just as you do when you call your family physician.

Calmly give an accurate description of your horse's symptoms: if he is standing or can't get up; if he is pacing back and forth or standing listlessly in a corner; if he is eating and eliminating normally; if he has a high temperature; or if the wound (in case of one) is bleeding, swelling, etc.

If your horse refuses to eat, check his feed and hay to see if they're wet, spoiled, or different than usual. Is his manure hard and dry or more liquidy? Is he restless, curling his lip, looking at his sides, rolling? Is he drinking water and able to urinate?

If he is lame, which leg is affected, how long has he been lame, and did it start before, during, or after work? Is his gait stiff?

Your vet will want to know his temperature (normal resting rate: 99–100 degrees Fahrenheit), pulse rate (normal resting rate: 28–40), and respiratory rate (normal resting rate: 8–16).

The temperature is taken with a rectal thermometer

made for livestock. Shake the mercury down and moisten or lubricate the bulb of the thermometer with petroleum jelly. Place the thermometer full length into the rectum and tie a 24-inch piece of string to the thermometer so you can secure it to the tail with a clip. This will keep you from losing it in the bedding if it falls out.

The pulse rate is the pulsation of blood through an artery caused by the heart's pumping. Take the pulse by feeling the artery that runs around the inner side of the horse's jaw.

The respiratory rate is the number of times per minute the horse inhales and exhales. Stand back and watch the in-and-out motion of the ribs, timing it with the second hand of your watch. Or place your hand on the ribcage or flank and feel the movement each time the horse breathes.

When your veterinarian does arrive, stay out of the way during the examination. If the vet asks you to hold your horse, try to keep him as still as possible by reassuring him with your voice and hands. If the veterinarian is unable to make a complete examination because your horse is too excited, a nose clamp or twitch may be used. It may look cruel to you, but remember that it is being used only for the good of your horse's health.

Be sure to follow faithfully all of your veterinarian's instructions regarding medication and treatment. Ask questions if you don't understand instructions or know how to follow them.

When you give your horse pills, the easiest way to crush them is with pliers. The smaller the particles, the more likely the horse will eat them. Mix the powdery material into grain or sweet feed with an ounce or so of corn oil so the powder will better adhere to the feed.

A great majority of all calls made by veterinarians are

the result of carelessness on the part of horse owners. To cut down on your horse's medical care—and even eliminate almost all but the annual boosters and vaccinations—you should feed your horse at the same time every day; give him a well-balanced diet in sanitary facilities; try to control the parasites around the stable and pasture area; keep your horse outdoors as much as possible, weather permitting; and exercise and groom him daily.

Gymkhanas, Events, and Shows

Small horse shows and gymkhanas can be all-day outings for the entire family: trailers, pickup trucks, and station wagons parked around the ring or in the shade of nearby trees; picnic lunches served on tailgates or spread out on blankets; horses everywhere—chestnuts, bays, blacks, and grays; and everyone participating either as competitor, photographer, groom, or spectator.

Local events, usually one-day affairs, can be found somewhere in your area almost every weekend throughout the summer months. Your neighborhood tack shop or riding stable will have brochures or posters on the bulletin board about upcoming events, and information may also be listed in local newspapers. Once you have shown a few times, you will probably be put on a mailing list and receive advance notification at home.

You will meet many of the same riders and their families again and again as you make the rounds of these smaller horse shows and gymkhanas, and you will have an excellent opportunity to make new friends with a common interest—horses.

The spring shows are exciting for everyone, but as the summer progresses, the weekly or biweekly hassle becomes tedious. By fall, parents, riders, and horses are exhausted. However, after a few months of winter's solitude, memories and friendships from the past summer will rekindle the flames of competition, and you will hardly be able to wait for the next show season to begin.

Horse shows are fun for both English and Western riders.

HORSE SHOWS

American Horse Shows Association (AHSA) events are "recognized" shows. Records of the results of their AHSA point classes are kept so that competitors can accumulate points for end-of-the-season awards and for eligibility to enter large shows, such as the Washington International Horse Show in Washington, D.C., or the National Horse Show at the Meadowlands in New Jersey. Riders trying to win these high-point AHSA trophies must show just about every weekend. It becomes very expensive and time-consuming, often more like a business than a pleasant pastime.

Other organizations, such as 4-H clubs, Pony clubs, area organizations, and charities sponsor "unrecognized" shows held at local riding stables, nearby fairgrounds, or in the open fields of a neighbor's farm."Unrecognized" shows are often smaller and more fun, with less tension than the larger ones, although the competition here can still be quite stiff.

Entry fees for recognized shows start at $25 for each class and must be mailed in advance. The small shows' entry fees start at $5 per class, and some shows may have a set fee for the day no matter how many classes you enter. These fees are usually mailed in advance or can be paid to the show secretary when you arrive on the day of the show. You may also be asked to sign a statement at this time releasing the show's sponsor and property owners from responsibility if you or your horse is injured.

Most shows and other events now require all horses and ponies to have written proof of a negative Coggins test from a veterinarian. This certificate is either sent in with the entry fees and returned the day of the show or is taken to the secretary's stand and returned when the competitor has finished showing that day.

Another fee, usually about $2, is a number fee, which is returned at the end of the day when you return the number that was assigned to you to wear in your classes. Some shows also charge an ambulance fee (about $4) to pay for an ambulance on the show grounds ready for any emergency.

There are many different kinds of shows and/or competitions for horses and their owners.

Breed Shows

Breed shows are held by associations such as the American Quarter Horse Association, the Appaloosa Horse Club, and the Morgan Horse Club. They sponsor shows to maintain the high quality of their breed by judging the entrants' ability, conformation (looks), and their way of moving. There are more shows for particular breeds in certain parts of the country: Saddlebred and Tennessee Walking Horse Shows are very popular in Kentucky and other parts of the South, while Arabian and Quarter Horse shows are held more often in the West and Southwest.

Hunter/Jumper Horse Shows

Hunter/jumper horse shows have three types of classes: equitation, or horsemanship, classes; pleasure horse and hunter classes; and jumping classes.

Equitation, or horsemanship, classes judge the riders on their position and their control of their mounts at various gaits "on the flat" or over a jump course. In pleasure horse or hunter classes the horse is judged for performance, conformation, way of going, manners, suitability, and soundness.

Jumping classes are judged solely on a horse's ability to clear designated jumps, whether trotting or galloping around the course. Scoring is on a mathematical basis. In "rub" classes, a hind foot touching or "ticking" a jump counts half a fault, a front foot one fault, knockdowns by hind or front feet two and four faults respectively; a third refusal, not following the proper course, falling by either the horse or the rider, or exceeding the time limit are immediate elimination. More often, the only faults are for knocking down the jump (four faults), and in "speed" classes the fastest time around the course wins in the event of an equality of faults.

Western Horse Shows

Western horse shows have four divisions: stock horse, trail horse, pleasure horse, and Western riding horse. In stock horse classes, if horses are not worked on cattle, they are required to perform a figure 8, sliding stops, spins, running at top speed, and backing. A trail horse shows his ability to walk, trot, jog, and lope over and through such obstacles as gates, bridges, water, and logs. They may also be asked to sidepass and to stand quietly while being mounted and dismounted from either side.

Pleasure horse classes require competitors to walk, jog, and lope both ways of the ring on a reasonably loose rein. They will also be asked to back in a straight line. Western riding horses walk, jog, lope and back in a pattern around markers set up in the ring to imitate the well-mannered,

A horse in a Western trail-horse class must be able to negotiate obstacles, such as crossing a bridge or opening a gate.

sensible, and easy-moving ranch horse who can carry his rider on the usual ranch chores.

The Dressage Show

The dressage show is another type of show that is growing rapidly in popularity throughout the United States. Publicity given to the United States' Olympics dressage squad introduced dressage to the public, and many riders like the preciseness and elegance of movements in the various levels of tests.

Many different breeds from this country—thoroughbreds, Arabians, Quarter Horses, and thoroughbred/draft horse combinations—and from European countries—Hanoverians, Oldenburgs, and Trakhaners from Germany and the Dutch and Swedish warmbloods, to name a few—compete against each other one at a time in a dressage arena. They show their willingness, roundness, and suppleness by doing a required routine or test, according to the level in which they are competing.

Levels range from Training Level, which introduces the horse and rider to the basic principles of dressage competition, to Grand Prix, where the competitors must do advanced movements such as canter pirouettes, flying changes of leads, *piaffe* (trotting in place) and *passage* (a highly collected trot). Smaller "unrecognized" shows may offer Green as Grass or Starter classes where beginners do their test only at a walk and trot.

There are also special classes for young riders (fifteen- to twenty-year-olds who will not turn twenty-one by December 1 of the current year) and juniors (youngsters who will not reach their eighteenth birthday by December 1 of the current year). They do the same routines as adults, but they compete only against their own age group.

The Driving Show

The driving show offers classes for adult and junior drivers of two- and four-wheeled vehicles. Pleasure driving competitions divide classes into ponies and horses and require the drivers to show their animals at a walk, pleasure trot, and road trot both ways around the ring, and to back when lined up. There may be driving games, such as Gambler's Choice, in which the drivers accumulate points by driving their horses through and around various obstacles, and a cross-country marathon.

Cutting Horse and Reining Shows

There are also cutting horse shows and reining shows. Cutting involves horses that perform by separating a steer from a herd and keeping him away from the others with little to no guidance from its rider. Reining horses perform a routine to illustrate a willingness to do various maneuvers, almost like a dressage show, Western style.

OTHER COMPETITIONS

Endurance Riding

Endurance riding tests the speed and endurance ability of the horse and the rider's knowledge of pacing his horse so they can finish the race in the fastest time in the best condition. An endurance race is run across the countryside—up and down hills, through streams, woods, and fields—and is from 25 to 100 miles long. The fitness of both horse and rider is very important. Most of the equine winners of this competition are Arabians or Arabian crosses.

Combined Training Events

Combined training events test the horse and rider in dressage, over a cross-country jumping course, and in stadium jumping. An event may be spread out over three days with a different test performed each day, or over two days or one day (called a horse trial). The riders ride the same horse throughout the event. There is a young riders' division for those competitors eighteen and under.

Vaulting

Vaulting, the art of gymnastics on a moving horse, resembles circus or trick riding. The rider is judged on the smoothness and execution of various exercises performed on the back of a horse circling on a longe line. There is team vaulting and individual vaulting. Team vaulting consists of compulsory exercises and a freestyle performance done by eight vaulters on one cantering horse. No more than three vaulters may be on the horse at one time.

Individual and *pas de deux* (two vaulters together) competitors must be at least sixteen years old to compete, while team vaulters must be under eighteen.

The American Vaulting Association was recognized by the AHSA (American Horse Shows Association) in 1987, so

Vaulting is the art of gymnastics on a moving horse.

it is the newest equine competition in this country. Over 250 competitors took part in the 1988 Nationals held in Sacramento, California. Most vaulting clubs are in California, but there are some scattered about in other states, too.

Gymkhanas

A gymkhana consists of "games on horseback," a kind of field day of fun events. Gymkhana riders compete against the clock as well as each other. The fastest time without a fault, such as knocking over a pole or barrel or stepping on the lines of the "keyhole" competition, is the winner.

Gymkhanas may also be "recognized" if they are members of the AHSA's Gymkhana Division. A fairly recent addition to the traditional horse show world, AHSA Gymkhanas have stricter rules than those in the sport's previous years. Bats, quirts, and crops are now forbidden, and tie-downs are restricted. The reasons for these and other changes in the rules were primarily for the rider's safety and the humane handling of the horses. It used to be a common occurrence to see riders hit their mounts the entire way around a timed event's course. The length of tie-downs is checked, because if they are too short, they can cause a horse to lose his balance and fall.

Some of the classes included in the AHSA Gymkhanas are the barrel race, pole bending, relay race, figure-8 stake, and the scurry (where a horse must go over three low jumps).

Other fun events are musical bags, egg and spoon, dollar bareback (in which you must not let a dollar bill slip out from between your knee and the horse's side while walking, trotting, and cantering bareback), "Simon Says," and costume competition. In this last class both horse and rider must be in costume.

Other Sports

Fox hunting is another equestrian sport. Hunting is more of a social ritual than a determined effort to kill foxes, and youngsters can enjoy a rich educational experience in cross-country riding while fox hunting.

Polocrosse is a game combining polo and lacrosse. Youngsters and adults, men and women, on all types of horses, from barrel racers to race horses to eventing horses, enjoy it.

Hunter paces or paper chases are for teams of two or three riders who follow a set route, picking up tokens at checkpoints and finishing in either the fastest time or closest to the ideal time.

Run, ride, and tie races have teams of one horse and two riders. The riders alternate riding and running until they cross the finish line. The first rider rides as far as he thinks the second rider can run, where he dismounts and leaves the horse tied to a tree. The second rider runs to where the horse is tied, mounts and rides to where he thinks the first rider can run, and so on until they finish the race.

WHY AND WHAT TO ENTER

Horse shows and gymkhanas are excellent measuring sticks of you and your horse's ability to work together as a team in competition with others. Whether you are jumping your horse 2 feet 6 inches, signaling him to begin a collected canter, or urging him on during a barrel race, the two of you should be partners, competing as one.

This partnership can hardly be formed in a day or two but must be built up over weeks of conditioning and practicing together. Find out what to practice by selecting the classes you wish to enter in an upcoming show and read up on their requirements. If it is a walk-trot-canter horsemanship class, you should walk, trot on both diagonals, and canter on both leads at home until both of you can perform these gaits perfectly together. One class may include dismounting and backing up, while another may add the hand gallop or riding without stirrups to its requirements, so you should always be prepared for a judge's request.

The current rule book on AHSA classes may be obtained from the American Horse Shows Association, Inc., 220 East 42nd Street, New York, New York 10017. It will list the different classes and their requirements as well as other information.

Your riding ability, your horse's or pony's training, and whether you ride English or Western will determine what classes are best for you. Go to a few nearby shows to see what the participants are asked to do in the classes you are interested in entering, and study the winners to see what they are doing to win.

Your riding instructor or a knowledgeable friend or parent ("knowledgeable" when it comes to assessing your horsemanship and your horse's ability for a certain class's requirements) can help you with this choice. Do not make the mistake of entering too many classes (three to five is the maximum), you will only wear out your horse. Your pet will be full of energy in the morning, but pooped out by the afternoon, so take this into consideration when deciding what classes to enter and the time of day when they are scheduled.

AWARDS AND PRIZES

Some horse shows use the democratic Danish system of judging, in which a rider competes, in effect, against herself. In any one given class there might be five blue (first-place) ribbons awarded or none at all. In another, everyone might get a red (second-place) or yellow (third-place) ribbon.

The much more familiar type of evaluation is one in which the judges pick the best, second best, etc., in the class against an ideal they have in their minds. "Ribbons" are the rosettes given to the best horse and rider teams and pinned on the winners' bridles. In addition to the first three colors are white (fourth-place), pink (fifth-place), green (sixth-place), purple (seventh-place), and brown (eighth-place).

SHOW PREPARATION

Set aside a definite time every day when you and your horse can practice. This will get both of you in condition as well as familiarize you with the routine of the classes you will be entering. Do not make these sessions too long or your horse will become bored. Several half-hour practices are better than one three-hour marathon. Vary the exercises. If you are planning to enter a jumping class, do not overjump your horse and make him weary of the whole idea.

If possible, try to get some instruction from a professional or an interested and knowledgeable friend at least to give you hints on how to show your horse to his best ability.

A knowledgeable instructor on the sidelines can see and tell you what you are doing wrong much more accurately than you can judge from the back of your horse.

For the best results, schooling should be done in an enclosed ring or field. Always shut the gate to prevent your horse from ducking out. Rather than going over and over the walk, trot, and canter, try figure 8s at a trot and then a canter, making sure to change leads in the center. Pull him back to a trot before changing leads in the center if you and your horse aren't familiar with flying changes.

Trot or canter and practice stopping to an absolute standstill. Trot over poles laid on the ground, back through two posts, and open and shut gates from your horse's back. Try sitting at a trot and then attempt all three gaits without stirrups.

Do a portion of your training and conditioning during a trail ride as a welcome break from the unavoidable drudgery that ring work can become, but do not relax to the point of sloppiness. It contributes to bad form and poor habits in both of you.

If your horse acts up when other horses are around, and you are planning on entering a horsemanship class where there will be plenty of company, invite some of your friends to bring their horses over or take yours to a nearby stable. Then practice the various gaits in a ring with horses alongside, behind, and passing you, so your mount becomes familiar with show-ring procedure.

A horse that is not well mannered at home will be worse in a show, so do not go expecting improvement. The highly charged atmosphere of a show ring puts even well-trained, steady horses on edge.

A good rider has complete control over the horse without a lot of shouting, arm-waving, and whip-lashing. Patience and understanding will go a long way toward correcting any bad habits or poor training your horse may have, but do not expect miracles overnight. Training and conditioning always take time. If you find yourself losing your temper, stop for the day, even if you have not worked for the allotted time you set aside.

To accustom your horse to traffic, lead him along a lightly traveled road, or stand him next to the driveway and have someone drive the car back and forth, or turn him out in a field next to a road. Be sure you have control over the horse in case he shies and tries to run away.

For your horse's safety, be sure the animal has had all of his inoculations and a current Coggins test (mentioned earlier in this chapter and in chapter 9) for equine infectious anemia. You may think that certainly entrants in horse shows are healthy—and they may even look that way to you—but there are carriers of disease even in the horse show world.

As an extra precaution, do not stand your horse next to another and allow them to rub noses. Do not let your horse drink from a public watering trough, or even graze where another horse has. Keeping your horse off in a corner, far away from any other horses, is a better idea.

JUMPING

If you are planning on entering a jumping class, take lessons from a professional and then practice at home only what your trainer suggests. A novice rider should never teach a horse to jump, and should always wear a hard hat (the kind recommended by Pony Club) when jumping.

THE DAY BEFORE THE SHOW

For the last few weeks you should have been giving special attention to your horse's coat so it now has a natural sheen. The day before the show give your horse a thorough cleaning—trimming whiskers and fetlocks, clipping ears and a bridle path, pulling the mane and putting in a little extra scrubbing on any white socks. Use Showsheen on the tail so tangles slip out when you brush it. Never yank and pull, breaking off hairs, or soon your horse will have a thin scraggly tail. For a white tail stained with manure and dirt, use a little diluted bleach or one of the special soaps on the market available in a tack store on the ends to whiten them.

If you are going to braid mane and tail, sponge them first, because wet hair is easier to plait. A little mousse on each section also makes the hair easier to work with. Use strong thread or yarn to hold the braids in place.

Put a sheet or light blanket on your horse for the night and keep him in the stall with extra bedding to prevent him from lying down in mud or manure. A few stains and smudges are unavoidable, but they can be quickly touched up in the morning.

Clean your tack and lay out your clothes. Try to look your best, eye-catching but not gaudy. You will have a much wider choice of colors and styles if you are dressing in Western clothes than in the more conservative English style.

Try to have colors of Western hat, shirt, and pants complement you and your horse. No red on a chestnut (too blah), but by all means, wear it on a black or gray horse for a striking combination.

Your hair should be neat and tucked in under your hat for the show. If it is long, put it in a braid, bun, or hairnet for the event because if your hair is flopping, you will look as if you are, too.

A clean, shiny horse and a neat, coordinated outfit are attributes for any riding competitor.

TRANSPORTATION

If you don't own a trailer, make arrangements well in advance for a friend to pick up you and your horse (you pay for the gas) or for a local rental firm or stable to transport your horse to the show. Depending on the distance you will be traveling, the vanning fee usually starts at $25.

If you live near the showgrounds, you can ride over, but be sure to arrive early enough for your horse to rest before the first class. If the trip is a long one, you may want to arrive the day before and stable your horse overnight. Be sure to make reservations early enough.

SHOW TIME

On the morning of the show, get up early and, wearing old clothes, water and feed your horse and muck out his stall, putting down a thick layer of clean bedding for him to enjoy upon his return after a tiring day at the horse show. After your breakfast, get dressed in your show clothes and put on an old jacket, an apron or oversized sweatpants or jeans, and rubbers to keep your clothes and freshly polished boots from getting dirty. A pair of old knit leg-warmers over your boots will keep them clean; push the foot end up to the ankles when you put them on and walk around. Some people prefer to get dressed at the show if they have a dressing room with their trailer.

Return to your horse in the barn and remove his blanket so you can brush out or sponge off any night stains. Then pick out his feet. To protect your horse's tail during trailering, wind a plain ace bandage from the top down to just above the end of the tailbone, and pin or tie it on the outside. A tail wrap with Velcro is even easier to use.

Wraps or shipping boots are needed to protect your horse's lower legs while traveling. If your shipping boots and wraps don't protect the coronary band of the hoofs, put rubber bell boots on for added protection.

Although show day may appear to be bright and sunny, experienced show-goers will bring umbrellas and other rain gear along with their folding chairs, blankets, and sun-shades.

In addition to saddle, bridle, halter, and lead shank, you should bring your own grooming equipment—brushes, cur-rycomb, old terrycloth, and most important of all, a hoof pick—for last-minute and periodic touch-ups during the day. An extra lead shank and halter will be greatly appre-ciated if your original is lost, broken, or stolen. Hay for your horse to nibble on throughout the day will alleviate your horse's boredom, and a bunch of carrots or other treats will be a welcome reward for good behavior.

A light sheet, essential to protect a sweating horse from drafts, will also keep him cleaner. Fly spray or fly wipe will drive off many of the flies that can irritate an already ner-vous horse to distraction. A first-aid kit for you and your horse is a good item to add to your gear, too.

Even if a show's brochure states that water is available, bring your own. Some horses are particular if it has an unfamiliar taste or odor, and lugging a bucket or two of sloshing water from the end of the showgrounds where the water is usually located to your trailer is hardly the way to keep yourself looking cool and clean.

Bring extra clothing in case an accident soils your original outfit. Remove your show jacket as soon as you dismount, and try to keep your horse from wiping his mouth on you. Apron and leg warmers, long skirt or baggy sweatpants should be put back on until your next class to eliminate the chance of dirt smudges on light-colored britches before and between classes.

A very important part of showing successfully is persuading someone to accompany you as your groom, either an unsuspecting relative or a very good friend. It may be a luxury, but it will be a very welcome one, to step off your horse at the end of a class and hand him to someone else to wipe off, untack, and lead around. You will be tired after a couple of classes, as much from the mental and emotional strain as the physical exertion, and very happy to pass the responsibility of your mount to someone else. It will also help you to keep your show clothes clean.

A groom is as important when you are on the horse's back as when you are off. Often, as soon as you mount, you will remember that you have forgotten to put on your number or that your gloves are in the car or that your horse is slobbering and needs his mouth wiped. What a pleasure not to have to dismount and then remount after you've tied or pinned on the number, fetched your gloves, or wiped your horse's mouth (knowing that he'll be slobbering again as soon as you remount).

Arrive at the showgrounds in plenty of time to park in a convenient spot, pay your entry fee, and pick up your number. Give your horse water and hay immediately, but take it away an hour before your first class when you get ready to warm him up.

Acquaint your horse with the new surroundings. Hubbub, crowds, other horses, and unfamiliar objects may be quite frightening at first, so you want the animal to get accustomed to all these distractions before you are under a judge's scrutiny. If you have entered a jumping class, let your horse watch the jumps being set up.

You will not be allowed to school in the main ring or over fences on the outside course if it is being used, but a horse that is unusually full of energy can let off some steam in the schooling ring or other areas set aside for exercising and warming up. Give him time to cool off and relax before your first class.

YOUR FIRST CLASS

When your class is called, mount up and give your boots one last flick of the dust cloth before entering the ring. Ring manners impress judges. Keeping a judge waiting while you saddle up when you should already be in the ring is a strike against you. As you enter the ring, go to your right and walk your horse counterclockwise along the rail. If others are in the ring already, going the opposite way, follow their lead. The judge or announcer will reverse everybody when they start the class.

Try to stay as calm and relaxed as possible because your reins will act as telegraph wires and send your every insecure signal to your horse. Your body should be flexible and supple, moving with your horse in all gaits. Be aware of the signals the horse gives you (pawing and fidgeting if nervous and excited, ears back if annoyed), so you can anticipate and correct any sudden move.

You are out to win and should use everything you know to achieve this goal, but do not forget courtesy and the rights of other competitors. If your mount starts to act up, pull out of line until you can quiet him. If he continues to misbehave, you will have to leave the ring so you do not jeopardize another's performance.

Be an individual and show your horse to his best advantage. Ride him the way he goes best, not necessarily the way the rest of the class is going. If he has a smooth fast trot, let him trot on, even if you do pass the rest of the horses. However, *you* decide, not the horse. You should be the boss.

Experienced competitors will give their horses plenty of room in which to work, avoiding ring congestion for several reasons. Most important of all is the safety factor. All horses have the potential to kick if crowded and nervous or excited. Another possible hazard is that other horses may affect your own mount's performance, with such moves as stopping suddenly in front of you just as you are passing in front of the judge in a collected canter. The judge will obviously get a better look at you and your horse if you are not crammed into a hodgepodge of horseflesh and other riders.

Slower horses should stay on the rail, so that the faster ones can pass on the inside.

If you find yourself boxed in, make a small circle at one end of the ring and move into line in an open area. You can also lose ground to the horses surrounding you by staying to the outside at the arena's ends (most horses take the shortcut across them) or gain ground by cutting off the ends completely. The ideal place is on the rail, with no other horses overlapping you.

When you are asked for another gait, make the change a smooth one with as little motion as possible. Flapping the reins, waving a crop, or drumming excitedly on the horse's sides with your heels does not make a pretty picture.

Your horse should be on the proper lead when asked to canter (inside front leg striking out first). If he is not, stop immediately and start him again until he is, even if you happen to be in front of the judge. This will make a better impression than continuing on the wrong lead.

Do not try to correct every little thing your horse does wrong. Your homework should be done at home, not in the show ring. Even if your horse is cantering in double time, give him a loose rein and keep a smile on your face as you pass the judge so he thinks you are in complete control. However, once out of his or her line of vision, take immediate action by pulling your horse back to a slower pace. Never show your temper or hit your horse. Both judges and spectators will disapprove.

When the judge asks all the horses to line up in the center of the ring for inspection at the end of the class, try to keep 5 feet between your horse and the ones on either side of you.

If you are not picked to receive a ribbon, congratulate those who have been and plan on doing better at the next show. Winning is an obvious desire of every competitor, but it should not overshadow everything else. Showing should be fun, and sportsmanship a part of horsemanship. If you have trained and conditioned both yourself and your horse to the best of your ability, and performed well during the class, then that is all you can ask.

The winner of a class is the best in one judge's opinion, and what one judge may dislike in one class could very well appeal to another judge in the next. Do not get discouraged. It may be you and your horse that will be "pinned" in the next class.

If you have entered the pole-bending event in a gymkhana, do not wear chaps or a wide hat. Either one can knock over a pole if you ride too close. Loose, flapping straps are also a hazard. Be sure your hat fits so that it does not fly off or fall down over your eyes. A pole is a lot easier to knock down than a barrel, particularly the end poles. Your horse must be trained not to get too close to them.

If you fall off, hang on to your reins and get up as quickly as you can to let everyone know that you are not hurt. However, if you think you might have injured yourself, stay still until you are sure you are all right. Later, do not hash over the incident with everyone, putting the blame on the horse, other riders, the jump, or the spectators. Just chalk it up to another experience you hope not to repeat.

AFTER COMPETITION

In between classes allow your horse to rest. Never leave him tied alone outside the van or car. Dismount, if you take your mount with you to watch some of the other classes; give his back a rest, and do not use it as a grandstand seat.

Loosen the girth a few notches, remembering to tighten it again before mounting. Do not lead your horse near parked cars, jostle spectators, or allow all your friends to take quick turns around the practice ring. Instead, spend your time wisely by watching other riders and seeing how the judge picks his winners. Try to pick out the winners in each class before they are announced.

After the show is over, get your horse home as quickly as possible. Trying to unload and take care of a tired horse in the dark is not fun if you are exhausted, too. Make sure he has fresh, thick bedding. Groom him thoroughly, and unbraid mane and tail to prevent the hairs from splitting or your horse from rubbing the braid out and chunks of his hair off. Give a good feed with fresh hay and clean water.

All of your hard work may someday pay off—a spot in the winner's circle and a ribbon pinned to your horse's bridle.

The constant round of shows and gymkhanas may eventually sour your horse on them, so follow a weekend of competition with a good rest.

If this did happen to be your lucky day and all your hard work paid off, remember that you are a team. Give credit to the other member of it, too—the horse in your backyard.

Bibliography

NATIONAL—ALL-INTEREST HORSE MAGAZINES

The Chronicle of the Horse (Weekly). Covers English riding sports, including horse showing, vaulting, grand prix jumping, fox hunting, steeplechase racing, dressage, endurance riding, driving, handicapped riding, combined training, polo, and Pony Clubs.

Equus (Monthly). Covers horse care, different breeds, equine illnesses and behavior, and training.

Horse & Rider (Monthly). Covers Western horsemanship and training, horse care, breeds, and stable management.

Horse Care (Monthly). Covers horse care, equine illnesses, injuries, and breeding.

Horse Illustrated (Monthly). Covers horse care, training, veterinary care, humor, and personal experience, as well as features on trends and issues in the horse industry.

Horseplay (Monthly). Covers horsemanship, stable management, competitions, and English horse sports including show jumping, dressage, combined training, fox hunting, and driving.

Horse Women (Eight issues per year). Covers women involved in the horse industry.

Horse World USA (Thirteen issues per year). Columns and articles on veterinary and horse care, nutrition, traveling, horse events, books and videos, and stable management.

Performance Horseman (Monthly). Covers Western riding: how-to and interview/profile.

Practical Horseman (Monthly). Covers English riding: how-to and interview/profile.

Western Horseman (Monthly). Covers Western horsemanship, training, rodeos, ranches, and Western historical articles.

There are also various specialized riding magazines, some of which are devoted to specific breeds.

RECOMMENDED HORSE BOOKS

Complete Book of Horse Care. Tim Hawcroft, New York: Howell Book House, 1983.

Effective Horsemanship. Noel Jackson, New York: Arco Publishing, 1967.

Encyclopedia of the Horse. Edited by Elwyn Hartley Edwards, New York: Crescent Books, 1977.

The Golden Book of Horses. George McMillan, New York: Golden Press, 1968.

Grooming to Win. Susan E. Harris, New York: Charles Scribner's Sons, 1977.

Horse and Horseman. Edited by Peter Vischer, New York: Arco Publishing, 1975.

The Horseman's Almanac and Handbook. Margaret Cabel Self, New York: Bonanza Books.

The Horseman's Catalog. Craig and Peter Norback, New York: McGraw-Hill, 1979.

The Horse Owner's Vet Book. E. C. Straiton, New York: Lippincott, 1973.

Horse Watching. Desmond Morris, New York: Crown, 1989.

Hunter Seat Equitation. George H. Morris, New York: Doubleday, 1971.

On Horses. Joan Embry and Robert Vavra, New York: William Morrow, 1984.

Rule Book. American Horse Shows Association, Inc., 220 East 42nd Street, New York, NY 10017; telephone (212) 972-2472.

The Whole Horse Catalog. Steven D. Price, et al., New York: Simon & Schuster, 1977.

Index